Naughty Medieval
EMBROIDERY

Naughty Medieval
EMBROIDERY

TANYA BENTHAM

THE CROWOOD PRESS

CONTENTS

INTRODUCTION

Medieval art is full of filthy images... except, is it really?

While I was writing this book I was visiting a primary school in my guise as Claudia Marcia Capitolina, a Roman lady, and one of the teachers was laughing because a delivery van had pulled up outside the office, complete with several penises scratched into the dirt on the back door. He thought this was amusing but completely inappropriate. I thought, 'It depends on how you look at it.'

Looking at it through modern eyes, it was both offensive and inappropriate. The person who defaced the vehicle could have done it for a laugh or because they thought the driver was a bit of a knob. However, if I looked at it through the Roman eyes of Claudia, I saw that some kind person had been so concerned for the welfare of the van driver that they'd taken the time to decorate his vehicle with some fertility symbols, thus ensuring the driver's happiness, the good health of his crops and the prosperity of his family.

It could have been done for all three reasons. All art – even the kind involving gratuitous genitalia, nudity and farting – is subjective and has different layers of meaning. Our ancestors (apart from the Victorians, who were such massive pervs they covered it up with a veneer of extreme prudishness) were just as amused by a good knob joke as we are today, but there were other layers of meaning to many of the images. You might be surprised how many of the images that inspired these embroideries have a religious connection... or, then again, you might not.

Some of the images are extremely rude; others are simply silly or a little strange. As with my previous books, I've arranged the projects with the easiest first and made each one a little more difficult as the book progresses. This book also offers an brief introduction to some of the other techniques of medieval embroidery – from convent stitch to whitework – all carried out with a rude twist.

The world's first unsolicited dick pic.

CHAPTER 1

MATERIALS AND EQUIPMENT

Unless you count the fact that I have multiple quantities of everything, I don't have a lot of 'stuff' for medieval embroidery. All you need is a simple frame, some scissors, a needle or three, and the right sort of threads.

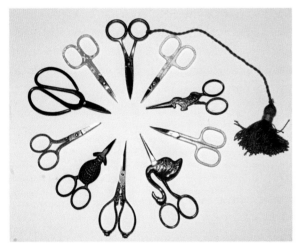

Obviously you need a pair of scissors, but you probably don't need this many pairs! I need these because my cat sits on them, forcing me to also have a decoy pair. Sometimes he can sit on the decoy pair and the pair and I'm using both at once, because he huge and fluffy, which is why I need all of the scissors.

Three living, three dead – set in an inner city because most young men don't go out into the country any more. This piece won the Innovative Use of Textiles category at the Fine Art Textiles Awards, 2022.

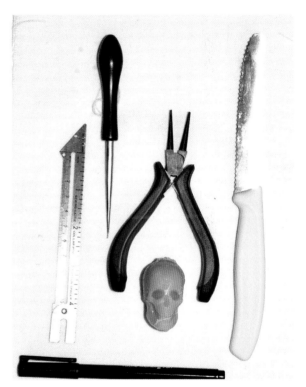

If you're absolutely desperate for more tools because tools make you happy (and, hey, who am I to judge?), this is about the extent of what I've got: beeswax for waxing linen; a serrated tomato knife for cutting notches into the side of cardboard thread tubes to anchor threads and stop them unreeling; a pair of pliers in case a needle gets stuck; a stiletto in case I need a bigger hole; a permanent fabric marking pen for patterns; and a buttonhole gauge, which I find quite useful for evenly spacing grid patterns like the one in the Danse Macabre project (see Chapter 5).

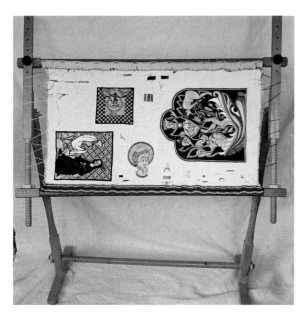

One of my floorstanding frames. (You don't have to work four projects at once, but when you're working on a book, it makes the photographer's life a lot easier!) My canvases are often chaotic because I doodle and experiment around the edges.

I have a proper slate frame for medieval demos, but to be honest I prefer these simple fixed frames because I'm forever losing the pegs on my slate and the sticky-out corners get on my nerves! My partner makes these by the dozen for when I'm teaching, and I tend to use them for small portable projects as well. Any decent woodworker should be able to knock something similar up quite quickly.

FRAMES

Hoops weren't a 'thing' in the medieval era; in fact, they turn up only quite recently in the history of embroidery, despite their current ubiquity. I don't recommend hoops at all. Even ignoring the difficulty of getting an even tension with a square-grained canvas on a round object, they just don't hold enough tension for most forms of medieval embroidery, especially for the opus anglicanum projects in Chapter 6, where tension is essential. So, do yourself a favour and ditch the hoop in favour of a frame, even if it's just a cheap artists' canvas with the canvas removed.

When I'm demonstrating medieval embroidery in costume, I use a pair of medieval trestles with a slate frame on top. The trestles are the same as those used for medieval table legs. They do the job well enough, but I don't use them at home because I find them too bulky and intractable. I much prefer the Elbesee C frame, with big wooden screws at the sides. These can be folded almost flat, so they're easily cleared out of the way. The screw sides give excellent tension, and they're light and easy to move around. I have seven, because simple doesn't mean you can't have more than one.

CANVASES

Evenweave Wool Canvas

I use evenweave wool canvas for most of my laid and couched work and Bayeux stitch. There is evidence for wool canvas in period work and it's an absolute joy to work on – so much nicer than working wool onto linen.

Ramie

I use this doubled for all of my opus anglicanum work. I like this canvas because it has a very high thread count (around 90), which allows for very accurate stitch placement. Also, it's very tough and will take no end of abuse. If I could find a linen with this thread count, I'd happily use it.

Linen

I never buy expensive linens. When I want to embroider on linen, I reach into the stash of fabrics that I use to make medieval underwear. They didn't really have evenweave canvas in the middle ages, they had 'it's even enough'.

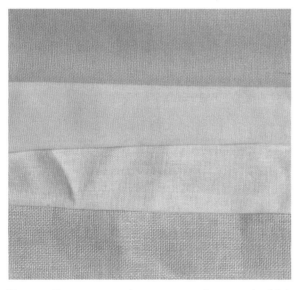

Top row: Evenweave wool canvas; second row: ramie; third and bottom rows: linen.

THREADS

Crewel Weight Wool

I use crewel weight wools that I dye using the same kinds of natural dyes that were available in the Middle Ages. I tend to refer to dark, medium or light madder colours. If you're using a commercially dyed product, it's fine to go a couple of numbers either side of the ones I give as equivalents in the Appletons range.

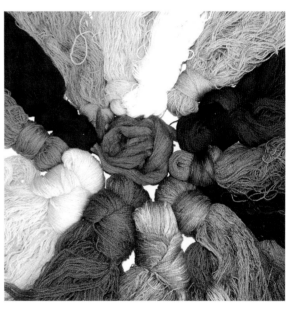

I dye crewel weight wools using the natural colours that were available in the Middle Ages – mainly madder, weld, woad, cochineal and walnut. The colours harmonise better than the modern aniline dyed kinds, and they are every bit as lightfast.

30/2 Silk

For the German brick stitch projects in Chapter 5, I used some 30/2 silks that I'd naturally dyed a few years ago.

The weight of 30/2 silks is a little heftier than a strand of standard embroidery cotton, and they're much softer.

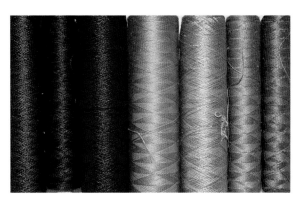

The same silks can also be commercially dyed, which I've used for the Zodiac Man (*see* Chapter 2).

Flat or Filament Silk

For the opus anglicanum projects in Chapter 6, flat or filament silk is essential. I would go so far as to say it's not opus anglicanum at all unless you use the right silk, because only filament silk brings light into the work. Japanese silks are also excellent.

The projects in this book are all done with DeVere silks. I use a mixture of 6 and 60, depending upon how many strands are required.

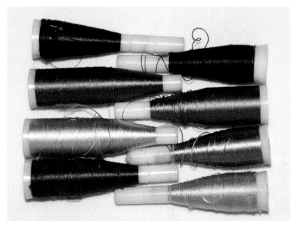

Sometimes you can also find old pirns of mill silks like these ones in flat silk. They're often cheap and nice to work with, but you have to be prepared to run out and not be able to replace the colours. They're a fantastic budget option, if you can find them.

Metal Thread

An essential element of opus anglicanum work is metal threads. In the Middle Ages, these would have been made from real gold and silver, but the modern alternative is passing threads, which are constructed in the same way, with a metallic outer wrapped around a thread core. Metal threads are available in traditional golds and silvers, as well as an exciting range of more modern metallic colours, which can be used to add an updated twist to the work.

Linen Thread

Linen threads have several uses and are not all equal in terms of strength.

I used metal threads for my Three Living and Three Dead piece, shown at the start of this section.

Cotton Thread

I use cotton thread for lacing my frames. A strong linen would be the medieval choice (and that's what I'd use for a demo when I want to be authentic), but cotton is more practical because it's cheaper and, more importantly, is far less susceptible to atmospheric moisture. (Linen stretches at the slightest damp in the air and I find myself constantly tightening the lacing when I use it.)

The white linen threads here are used for the whitework pieces in Chapter 7. I use the yellow for the 'under' part of underside couching in opus anglicanum (see Chapter 6). It should never show on the surface, so the colour is irrelevant; what matters for the underside is the strength of the thread, as it takes a lot of abuse.

This is perle 5 cotton (which is also sold for crochet under the name DMC Petra in bigger skeins and at a fraction of the price of the embroidery version). It's worth keeping two colours on hand in case you want to overlace a frame – you can lace in a second colour and know which threads to tighten without having to completely unlace the canvas.

CHAPTER 2

STEM STITCH

tem stitch is one of the world's oldest stitches, used by some of the oldest-known embroideries, from the Llangors textile of Iron Age Wales to the Paracas mummies of pre-conquest South America.

Modern embroidery makes a distinction between stem and outline stitches on the basis of whether you take your needle to the top or bottom of the line. As someone who struggles with direction, I find this utterly confusing, not to mention pointless, because if you turn the stitch 180 degrees it's all the same anyway.

STEM STITCH METHOD

When stitching, make sure the stitches are on the same straight line to ensure that the finished row of stitches has a smooth, rope-like appearance.

1 Bring your needle out at the start of your line.

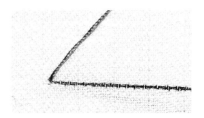

2 Take the needle down about 4–5mm (¼in) along the row, then come back up halfway along the previous stitch.

3 Each stitch should be roughly the same length and should overlap the previous stitch by half its length, so you will only progress half a stitch length with each subsequent stitch.

4 It is tempting to try and make the work go quicker by stretching the stitches out and not going all the way back, but as you can see this makes for a straggly, uneven row.

5 Compare the stretched row at the top with the properly overlapped row at the bottom – the difference is apparent.

The modern witch likes to keep up with the latest gadgets.

Troubleshooting

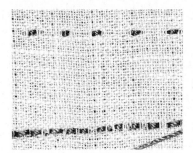

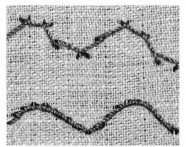

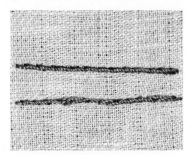

I'm not one to obsess over the appearance of the back of the stitches, but in many cases, seeing what the back should look like helps us to understand how the stitch works. Here you see the bad stem stitch at the top, which looks like an uneven row of dots. The good example at the bottom looks a lot like conventional backstitch

The difference between the good and the bad become even more evident once you start to introduce some movement to the line.

It's also important to remember direction with this split. Always go above or always go below; you can't mix the two or you end up with a wobbly line. The upper line has all the stitches to the same side, making a straight, even rope. The lower line has several changes of direction along its length and you can see how uneven it has become.

STEM STITCH PROJECTS

Wheee!

She looks very po-faced for someone riding an enormous green willy, doesn't she? This image is taken from a marginal illustration in the *Decretum Gratiani* of 1340. I've worked it in stem stitch in a fairly open, sketchy style to reflect the feel of the original drawing.

You'd think she'd be a bit more pleased with herself, all things considered.

Materials

- Linen canvas, 30cm (12in) square
- Crewel needle, size 22
- Silk 30/2nm threads:
  - Dark brown
  - Green
  - Flesh pink
  - Pink
  - Brown

Transferring the Design

If you're using a permanent marker, as I tend to, make sure it has a fine line so you can completely cover it.

Wheee! template, actual size.

Colour map.

1 Transfer your design to the canvas.

The Flying Penis

He's got quite a friendly face, so try to give him a nice smile. If you met an enormous flying green phallus in reality you probably run a mile (or at least I would) so it's probably best to make him look as unthreatening as possible.

Really, if you think about it, riding a big green willy isn't all that different to riding around on any other phallic symbol.

2 Work the outline of the flying penis in a single line of dark brown. It looks nice if you add some little furry tufts to its ears.

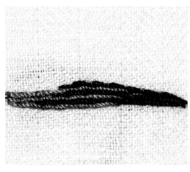

4 In places where you want more depth to the layers of stem stitch, say around the testicles, you can use a layering technique to thicken the line smoothly. I've worked it here in two colours so you can see more clearly. Work about two-thirds of the way along the row, then double back over the central portion. This way, the ends will be single rows while the centre doubles in width.

3 The next stage is simply a case of working around the inside of the brown with several layers of green, making sure to pack the rows nice and close together. I've done between three and four rows, but you can do more or less according to your personal taste (although if you're currently embroidering an enormous green todger, it might be a good time to question your personal taste, to be honest. I mean, I've been a lost cause in that regard for decades, but you might still be able to save yourself if you put this book down right now and run away).

The Rider

Add some shape to the rider's body by using spirals of stitch to outline the large areas of muscles. This is much the same principle used to fill in the flesh areas in the Hellmouth project in Chapter 6.

5 Outline the rider's body in a single row of dark brown. Leave her hair.

6 Use spirals of stitch in flesh pink to outline her lovely fat thighs.

7 Use the same spiralling technique to add shape to her lower leg and arms.

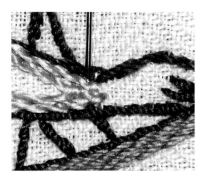

8 Bring the needle out right out of the join between the spiral and the outline. It's important to come out quite far to get the stitches to blend well.

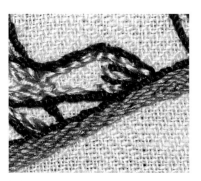

9 Work down the sides of the hand and fingers.

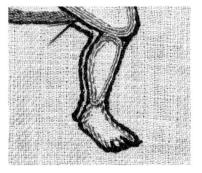

10 Do the same for her feet, before coming out and filling the shadowed rear leg.

11 The rest of the body is simply worked by shadowing the dark outline with a flesh-coloured one.

12 It's best not to overwork the face, lest it begins to look clunky, so simply outline the apple of the cheek, the brow and the nose.

13 Add just a hint of pink lippy, because it is oh so very important to look one's best when riding an enormous green todger.

14 Her hair is rather elegant (I suspect she's used a lot of product to get it to stay put during her exertions), but the braid is really just a series of small interlinked 'S' shapes in brown.

15 Off she goes!

Zodiac Man

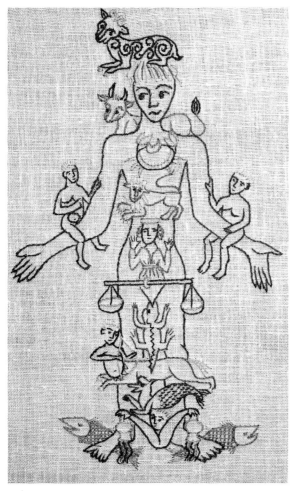

Zodiac Man.

Based on a Byzantine zodiac document, I love how the sun in the middle looks so hungover.

The Zodiac Man isn't as rude as his companion in this section on stem stitch, since all his rudey bits are covered up, but I admit I have a soft spot for him and for a lot of medieval zodiac characters. Mine is based on John of Arderne's fifteenth-century text, *Mirror of Phlebotomy & Practice of Surgery* (Glasgow University Library, MS Hunter 251 (U.4.9), folio 47v).

The modern world largely regards the zodiac as mythology, but in the medieval world it was an accepted science. The Zodiac Man was a diagnostic tool for physicians and surgeons. He shows which part of the body is governed by which sign, and a large part of his use was to give guidance on whereabouts bloodletting was to be done in conjunction with the phases of the moon. Some versions even cheerily illustrate blood pouring from the various letting points. (Mind you, if he's meant to be a diagnostic tool, you'd think the first thing any decent physician ought to notice is that there's a scorpion trying to bite his knackers off.) He's really little more than a needle sketch and is a great way to practise your stem stitch with an easy weekend project, but you could also use him as the base for a more detailed treatment.

I would urge you to be conservative with the number of colours you use here. I've chosen a set of colours dictated

Colour map.

Zodiac Man template. Enlarge by 200%. Finished size 30 × 40cm (12 × 16in).

by those associated with each sign, but each colour is used more than once throughout the image to create harmony. If you use a colour only once in an image it will stand out. Sometimes that can be what you want, but most of the time it's just jarring to the eye. Medieval embroidery tends to be very limited in the range of colours used, and sticking to this ethos will help your work look authentic. I haven't listed exact colours, as I think this is a great stash-busting project to use up odds and ends.

We will work in split stitch throughout, unless otherwise stated. I'm going to work down the body from his head, showing one sign at a time.

Materials

- Linen canvas, 30 × 40cm (12 × 16in)
- Crewel needle, size 22
- Medium-weight threads – I've used silk 30/2 nm threads, but any cotton or silk thread would work in the following colours:
  - Brown
  - Yellow
  - Orange
  - Red
  - Deep pink
  - Black
  - Bright green
  - Chestnut brown
  - Royal blue
  - Sky blue
  - Pale grey-green
  - Purple

Zodiac Man Outline

Notice that I haven't marked the heads and hands of some of the smaller characters in great detail in this project. Part of the charm of a piece like this is its sketchy nature, which adds a kind of immediacy to the image. Fingers, toes and hair can be indicated by tiny lines that really don't need to be marked out accurately.

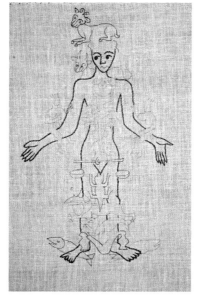

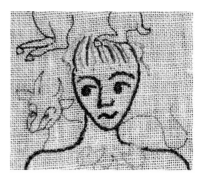

1 Transfer your design onto the canvas. I've used a permanent fabric marker, but have deliberately chosen one that's running out and leaves a faint line because the embroidery will not be very thick. However, you could use a slow-fade or wash-out pen if you prefer.

2 Mark the outlines of the Zodiac Man's body and face where they will show in brown thread. This really isn't much, but working it first allows the signs to sit on top of him.

3 My Zodiac Man is going to be a floppy blonde, indicated by alternating stripes of yellow and orange, but you can give yours any colour hair you like. His mouth is worked in red, and I love that it's an uncertain looking little squiggle, like he's really none too sure about what's going on here.

Aries

The little lamb governs the head and eyes, which is why he is pretending to be a rather natty little hat.

4 Start by working some scrolling spirals in deep pink to represent the lamb's fleece. I haven't marked these on the template because they don't have to be accurate. Just have fun with them, keeping your stitches small so the curves are smooth.

5 Outline the lamb in red.

6 Work the hooves and horns in yellow. The hooves are so tiny, you can use a few satin stitches. His eyes are simply little dots of black satin stitch.

Taurus

Taurus is in charge of the neck and throat, so he takes the role of warm scarf.

7 Taurus is an earth sign, so outline him in bright green. Note that the top of his head, where he has a little bit of a wig, is denoted by a simple series of stab stitches where the pattern was blank.

8 His horns and tail are deep pink and his eyes are a nice moo-cow brown.

Gemini

Gemini is in charge of the shoulders and arms. On some zodiac men, this sign is shown as two elegantly clad ladies, but in this book we have the more normal depiction of Gemini as two naked boys. I love the way they're feeling his muscles – you can just hear them cooing, 'Ooh, mate, have you been working out?'

9 Gemini's dominant colour is yellow, which is a bit weak for an outline, so I've used chestnut brown instead. Again, note that the fingers and toes are indicated by a few small lines at the open ends of the limbs.

10 Bring in the yellow for the spiky hair, again filling in the gaps at the top of each head.

Cancer

Cancer, the crab, rules the chest. Considering the amount of fish demanded by the medieval religious diet, your average scribe is rubbish at drawing crabs, and they often end up looking more like head lice. This one is relatively realistic, all things considered.

11 Outline the body and arms in royal blue.

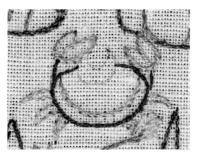

12 Work the claws, legs and inner line of the shell in sky blue. I didn't mark the small legs on the pattern because, like hair and fingers, they are easily indicated by simple lines.

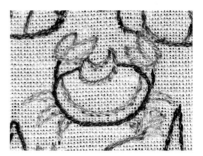

13 The eyes of medieval crabs are always indicated by a little half-moon shape, in this case worked in grey-green.

Leo

Leo, the lion, governs the sides and heart, making our Zodiac Man lion-hearted.

14 Outline the lion in orange.

15 His wig is a little zigzag of yellow. His mane and tail are a series of leaf shapes, while his claws are optional little stab stitches. Give him eyes of black or brown.

Virgo

Virgo is in charge of most of the internal squishy bits, so she sits on the belly.

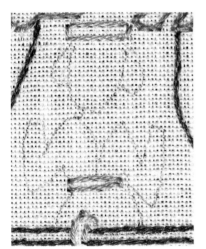

16 Work Virgo's hat and belt in pale grey-green.

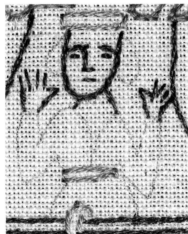

17 I've worked her hands and face in chestnut brown because she is an earth sign. I didn't mark out her hands because they're just a series of stab stitches.

18 Virgo's dress and hairnet are bright green. Like the fingers, the creases in her dress are best left to fill in randomly. Her hairnet is outlined in stem stitch, with a small cross in the middle to indicate netting.

Libra

Libra is in charge of the arse. You might think this is a little odd, but start looking into medieval medical texts and you will realise that they were obsessed with anal fistulas and diarrhoea, so to have a bum sign makes sense. (And I suppose you could say that the pans look a bit like two bum cheeks?) To save the poor zodiac chappie from some painful contortions, this is shown on the lower stomach.

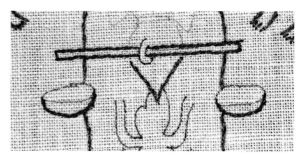

19 Outline the balance beam and the lower half of the pans in royal blue.

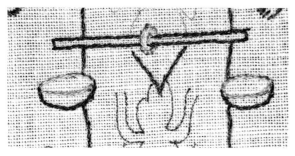

20 Then outline the pivot of the beam and the upper part of the pans in sky blue.

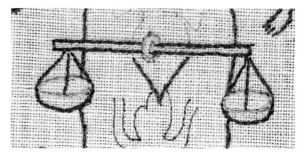

21 Finally add the chains to connect the pans to the scales in bright pink. This is another part of the design that is easier to just fill in, rather than following a marked line.

Scorpio

Scorpio is in charge of the genitals, and this particular Scorpio looks very much in charge of our Zodiac Man's genitals – no wonder he's got such a funny look on his face! And yes, he does look more like a tiny crocodile, but whoever drew this had almost certainly never seen a scorpion.

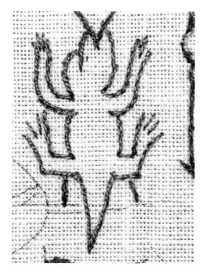

22 Outline the scorpion in purple.

23 Add a zigzag ridge down the scorpion's back and an eye in black.

Sagittarius

Sagittarius is governor of the thighs, and he's a little elongated to stretch across them both.

24 Outline the animal part of Sagittarius in his dominant colour, purple.

25 Use black to outline the human part of him. He is so tiny that his fists are just tiny blobs – don't stress about making them realistic.

26 His final colour is yellow for some spiky hair, some satin-stitched hooves, his bow and arrow, and a tail indicated by a few simple lines. The body of his recurved bow is the only place I've used a double row of stem stitch to add contrast to the single lines of the bowstring and arrow.

Capricorn

Capricorn is often a goaty little sea-monster in medieval zodiacs. He is charge of knees, so I suppose making him a bit fishy means he is water on the knees.

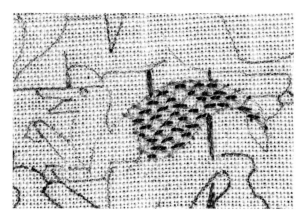

27 Work Capricorn's tail in open trellis stitch using pale grey-green for the trellis and black for the couching points to give a scaly fishtail effect.

28 Work an outline of chestnut brown around the goat's body and tail.

29 Add the finishing touches of the hooves, back of the ear and eye in black. Like hair, the tailfin is best worked freehand.

Open Trellis Stitch

Open trellis stitch is similar to the trellis stitch used in the laid and couched work projects in the next chapter. In this case, no background laidwork is used and the canvas shows through the stitching.

Simply work diagonally to make a row of long stitches in a single strand of silk, then work over them at right angles to create a net. Work to the edges of the space you wish to fill.

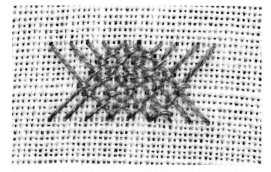

Secure this loose net of stitches by stitching over each intersection. You can do this with either a contrasting or toning colour.

Pisces

Aquarius should come next in the strict sequence of zodiac signs, and in the order they're shown on the body, but we're going to do Pisces first so Aquarius can sit on top of the fishtails. Zodiac Man is surfing on fishes because Pisces is in charge of feet.

30 Work the fish bodies in bright green trellis with sky blue points to give a shimmery, watery look.

31 Outline the faces and bodies in bright green.

32 Like the hair and fingers of the other signs, the fins are best worked freehand, in this case using sky blue.

Aquarius

Aquarius governs the shins and is just a torso – we've stitched him last so the water can flow over the fishes' tails.

33 Outline Aquarius's tunic in royal blue, give him a couple of piercing blue eyes, and then work some wavy lines of water pouring out of the two vessels. Make sure to leave room for extra water lines in our next colour.

34 Work his hands and facial details in black.

35 Finally, work the pots in sky blue, shaping them by working a central circle with the neck and base coming out from it. Give him sky blue hair and add some extra water lines in between the royal blue ones.

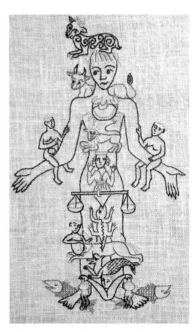

36 Here is our final Zodiac Man, naked but well-covered.

CHAPTER 3

LAID AND COUCHED WORK

This is a very easy stitch, which is great for filling large areas quickly. It's often associated with the Bayeux Tapestry and is sometimes known as Bayeux stitch, but I prefer the name laid and couched work because the stitch was used throughout the Middle Ages for much more than the Bayeux Tapestry.

In this chapter, the Bayeaux Rudies project is worked the Bayeux way by doing the outline first and the filler last. I've worked the filling first for the Bonacon project – it's faster to work this way and seems to have been the standard method in later pieces. It's also much easier for a beginner, since working the outline second allows you to cover a multitude of the kind of mistakes a beginner will make.

LAID AND COUCHED STITCH METHOD

Whether you start in the middle or along the edge of the shape you are filling will depend upon the shape. With a square it's easier to begin along one of the edges, but with circles and irregular shapes you may find it easier to start in the middle and work out, as I have done here. If, like me, you mark your canvas with a permanent marker, work a fraction to the outside of the line so that you cover it (all of the laid and couched work patterns in this book are intended to be worked slightly to the outside of the line).

The laid and couched method of working makes sense in a medieval context, where not only were many of the dyes expensive and time-consuming to produce, but also spinning thread fine enough to make an embroidery wool would be a skilled job. This method makes the most of the resources available by keeping them all as visible as possible. As well as being very economical with thread, this method also reduces a lot of bulk from the work so that the finished product lies neatly.

Bonacon – as with most serial farters, he looks quite pleased with his efforts.

1 Using two strands of crewel wool doubled over, stitch across the entirety of the space to be filled.

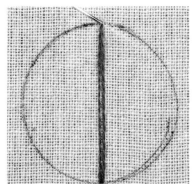

2 This isn't satin stitch, so don't carry the thread over the back, but rather bring the needle up, right next to where you took it down. All of the thread should be on the surface and you only need to move one thread of the background canvas along. Sometimes you will pop the thread back out of the hole and have to start again, but that just means you're packing the laid work close enough together.

3 Cover the whole area in this way.

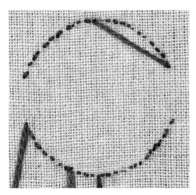

4 The back should have hardly any stitching showing, apart from a tiny row of stab stitches around the edge.

5 Normally you would do the next stage, the couching, in the same coloured thread, but I'm using a contrasting colour for added visibility. (There are examples of a contrasting couching thread used in period to create a pattern, but they are the exception rather than the rule.) The laid threads are still quite unstable, so take a single thread and lay a bar across the laid threads at a right angle.

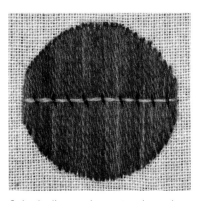

6 Again, I've used a contrasting colour for added visibility. The bar on its own is no more stable than the laid work, so work over it with a row of whip stitches, after which it will sit still.

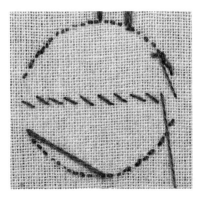

7 The back of the bar will show as a row of stitches inside the area of the edges. I strongly recommend couching each bar as you lay it down, as this will help you evenly space the bars. So go back and forth along the bar, rather than putting lots of bars down and couching them all at once, especially when you are a beginner.

8 As you lay down subsequent sets of bars, try to couch them at roughly 4mm (⅛in) intervals, with the couching stitches also about 4mm (⅛in) apart. This spacing will give a good stable surface to the stitch. The couching stitches should also be slightly staggered, rather than lined up.

Troubleshooting

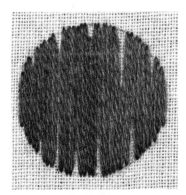

One common problem that beginners have with this stitch is not packing the laidwork tightly enough together. Often, this problem won't really become apparent until you start to couch, when the couching points will push the laidwork apart in any sparse areas, but all is not lost.

Simply take a double strand of wool (I've used a contrast colour so you can see the fix) and slide in from the edge to fill the gap. You'll need to duck under each couching bar so as not to disrupt the texture. It's best to go further in than you think you need to, so the threads blend seamlessly.

Laid and Couched Stitch Projects

The finished piece makes a nice cushion.

Materials

- Linen or wool canvas, approx. 38cm (15in) square
- Crewel needle, size 18
- Crewel wool:
  - First madder/coral 866
  - Second madder/coral 863
  - Weld/bright yellow 554
  - Weld/woad green/grass green 254
  - Woad/sky blue 566
  - Compound black/charcoal 998
  - Compound brown/chocolate 187
  - Fustic/autumn yellow 476

Colour map.

Bayeux Rudies

The little creatures and people frolicking along the margins of the Bayeux Tapestry are by far my favourite part of that work. Sometimes, like the poor warrior being stripped of his armour that I've reproduced here, they support the main plot, but often they're just pottering around doing their own thing and letting history take care of itself. The little naked people in the Bayeux Tapestry have often been overlooked or deliberately erased – the Victorian replica in Reading Museum prudishly erases any visible genitalia – so I've given them their own central stage in this design. You can work all five together or use the patterns for smaller projects.

Bayeux Rudies template. Enlarge by 200%. Finished size 38cm (15in) square.

For this project I'm working by doing the outline stitches first, which is the method of the original tapestry, but this can lead to problems when covering the areas of laid work up to the edges. If you prefer to do the laid and couched section first then do so; it's what I normally do. I have used naturally dyed wools, so I will list the name of the dye plus the equivalent in number in Appletons wools. None of the colours used was more than a skein and several colours were only a metre or two; with a judicious change of colour here and there. This would be an ideal project to use up bits and pieces from other projects – it's definitely a project where my colours are just suggestions!

The Framework

Remember that this technique works best if you have the canvas under good tension, preferably drum tight, so it's best to work both the stem stitch (*see* page 15 for stem stitch instructions) and the laid and couched work under the same tension for a consistent result. Use two strands of wool for the stem stitch outline to give it a bit more oomph – we will go down to a single strand later for the figures. I based this framework on the diagonal lines in the margins of the Bayeux, but they've come out with a pleasingly art deco feel.

1 Transfer your design to the canvas.

2 Work around the outer edge in two strands of first madder/coral.

3 Medieval textiles don't really feature monochrome outlines (just look at the Bayeux Tapestry), and it's one of the things that will make your work look instantly modern. I used second madder/coral for the trapezoid boxes around the edge, but blues and green would look pretty fabulous too.

4 Use weld/bright yellow for the inner box and the corners.

The Corners

Now that the framework is in place, go down to using a single strand of wool for the stem stitch. The trailing vine design in the corner is adapted from several examples in the Bayeux Tapestry, but I've added a little willy instead of a flower at the end of the vine to blend it in with our theme.

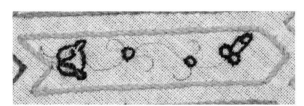

5 Begin by outlining the lion's head, small circles and willy in first madder/coral. The example shown is stem stitch but you may find you get better definition with split stitch, so it's worth trying both.

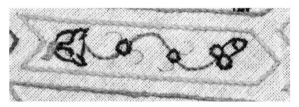

6 Use a small length of second madder/coral for the cat's tongue, and work the vine in green.

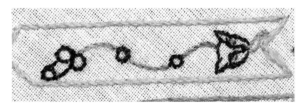

7 I couldn't decide whether the cat's eyes would look better in blue or green, so I did two of each in diagonally opposite corners.

8 Add a little flourish of woad/sky blue for the tendrils. Whether you decide to add an extra splash of blue inside the circles is up to you, but it's a nice contrast to the yellows and oranges.

Naked Yoga Chappie

In my imagination, this chap is a colonel with the British East India Company, sometime during the days of the Raj. There's just something quite pompous about him – perhaps it's the handlebar moustache? I think he's started doing his daily stretches in the nude because he forgot to wear his pith helmet and caught a touch of the sun, but he'd better hope there aren't any man-eating tigers out there who fancy a bite of his sausage! I'm sure he meant something quite different to the original artists of the tapestry, but that's who he is in my head!

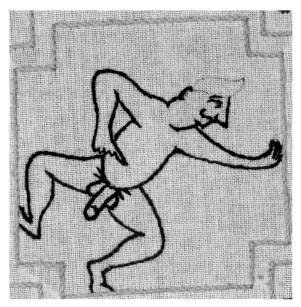

9 When I dye my own threads, black is a complicated colour requiring many stages. Because I'm not the world's best dyer, it can be a little hit and miss, landing anywhere between charcoal and chocolate brown. Therefore, I've chosen to use two colours for his dark outline (compound black/charcoal and compound black/chocolate), mixing them randomly according to where and when the thread in my needle ran out.

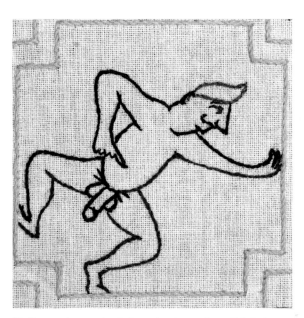

10 I've used a touch of ginger for the outline of his hair to add warmth.

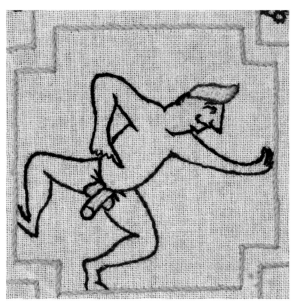

11 Fill his hair and his willy with laid and couched work in weld/bright yellow. Take care to tuck the laid work right underneath the outline so that no gaps show. It's probably best not to ask why he has a bright yellow todger...

The Ill-Advised Chopper

That's just not going to end well, is it? Time and time again, the Bayeux Tapestry illustrates the blatant lack of regard for basic health and safety in the Middle Ages. He probably has a ridiculous name for the axe as well, like the one that was given to our re-enactment group, which the boys unanimously named 'Big Willy'. I think in this case 'Big Willy' could well end up with him having a much smaller, and probably very ouchy, willy.

12 Outline his body and the axe in either compound black/charcoal or compound brown/chocolate. As with the previous figure, I've used a mixture of the two.

13 Outline his hair and penis and the chopping block in first madder/coral.

14 Fill the hair and chopping block with laid and couched work in second madder/coral.

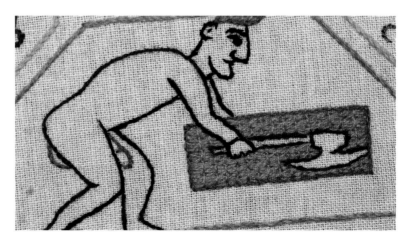

Not Tonight Dear, I Have a Headache

She doesn't look keen, does she? I have edited this one a little bit, because in the original she has black hands that stand out a great deal, like little gloves – maybe her paramour has a glove fetish?

15 Outline the man's body (but not his head) in compound black/charcoal or compound brown/chocolate.

16 His hands are still quite glove-like when outlined in first madder/coral, but this is common in these marginal figures. Outline her body, his willy and the back of his neck in the same colour.

17 Outline his face and both sets of hair in fustic/ autumn yellow.

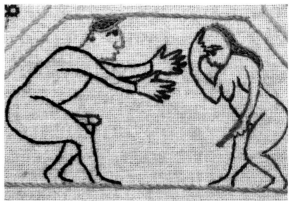

18 Fill their hair with a spot of laid and couched work. In the original they both have orangey madder-coloured hair, but I've used woad/sky blue to balance the blue tunic on the stripper panel, which lies opposite.

Pointing at Naughty Bits

The man's moustache highlights the fact that he's a bit of a bounder, because obviously this game is mainly played by under-sevens.

19 Use compound black/charcoal or compound brown/chocolate to outline the front part of the woman's body, the man's hair and his impressive handlebar moustache.

20 Outline the rest of their bodies in first madder/coral.

21 Her hair is outlined with just a splash of fustic/autumn yellow.

22 In the original, the woman's hair is simply outlined and left empty, but because that would leave this as the only panel on my cushion without an area of laid and couched work, I've filled her hair with first madder/coral to balance the design.

Stripper

This is one of the marginal panels that tells a more immediate story relating to the main narrative above. Many naked dead are shown in the process of having their armour stripped from them as part of the spoils of war; a perfectly respectable way to get yourself some shiny new stuff if you were on the winning side. Despite the grisly subject matter, there is a lovely sense of movement here, almost as if the naked figure has tripped and fallen out of his armour.

23 Outline the naked figure, as well as the eye and one of the legs of the other figure, using compound black/charcoal or compound brown/chocolate.

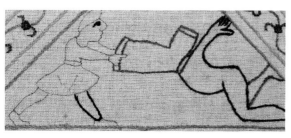

24 The armour is outlined in second madder/coral.

25 And the rest is outlined in fustic/autumn yellow.

26 Use woad/sky blue to fill the body of the armour with tightly packed spirals of split stitch to represent the chain mail. Small circles can be difficult, so if you look at pages 32–33 of my book *Bayeux Stitch* you will see a visual study of the different ways of representing armour in the Bayeux Tapestry. There are a couple of easier options, as well as some that are more complicated.

27 Fill the collar and cuffs of the armour, as well as the clothed figure's legs and hair, with first madder/coral.

28 Finish by filling the tunic with woad/sky blue, taking care to tuck the laid work right under the stem stitch outline so no gaps show. The original figure had empty feet, so I've left them empty here too,, but you can fill them with a spot of whatever colour you have handy, if you prefer.

Bonacon

The Bonacon is named Malcolm, after my dad, who has much the same talent.

The Bonacon is a mythical beast that time seems to have been forgotten. He appears in nearly every medieval bestiary, and I think he's due a revival. This particular example is from the bestiary of the second family, MS Ashmole 1511, c.1200.

The Bonacon is always a he because he takes the form of a bull. Due to the inward curve of his horns, he is unable to defend himself in a normal bullish fashion so instead he uses an early form of chemical warfare by farting an enormous toxic cloud at his enemies. Some sources say this cloud can extinguish all life for several miles around.

I'm embroidering a Bonacon in honour of my dad, who is not only a Taurus, the astrological sign of the bull, but who also has a similar tendency to produce toxic fart clouds. Maybe my dad's efforts might not actually be able to extinguish life, but they can certainly make any life forms they encounter wish for death. So my Bonacon is named Malcolm, in honour of my dad, but I'm pretty sure we all know a latter-day Bonacon and you may name yours after whomever you wish.

Fart jokes were quite popular in the Middle Ages. Roland le Fartere was a jester at the court of King Henry II, who was given a farm in exchange for performing a jump, a whistle and a fart at the Christmas feast, and even livestock were depicted getting in on the fun. (It amuses me more than words can say that Latin for fart is *bombulum*. I only just learned that looking up Roland and I shall use it as much as possible from now on.)

Fart pony.

Toot toot!

Colour map for laid and couched work.

Bonacon template. Enlarge by 400%. Finished size 45 × 30cm (18 × 12in).

Colour map for outline.

This project will expand upon the technique of laid and couched work, or Bayeux stitch, which was used throughout Europe during the entire Middle Ages. In this case, we will work the laid and couched work first and add the details in stem and split stitch afterwards. I've used naturally dyed crewel wools (again, I will give both the dye name and the closest Appletons colour) and a woollen canvas, but the design covers most of this – I find wool on wool is far more pleasant to sew.

Split Stitch

1 Bring the needle out from the back of the canvas, and make a straight stitch of about 4mm (just over ⅛ inch). Bring the needle back up again about halfway along the first stitch, splitting it in two – hence the name split stitch.

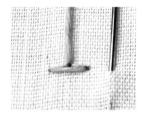

2 The second and subsequent stitches should all be about the same length as the first, but half of each stitch should overlap the one before, so that each stitch advances by only half its length.

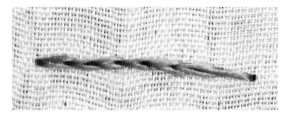

3 By keeping each stitch the same length and covering half the previous stitch you should end up with a smooth, even row of stitches.

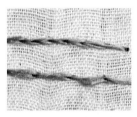

4 It can be tempting to stretch out the stitches to make things go quicker, by making each stitch longer and not going all the way back to meet the one before, but as you can see here the results are messy. The upper row is smooth and even, made from seven stitches, whereas the straggly mess below makes a longer row from only four stitches.

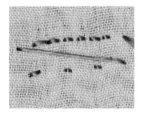

5 Turning the stitches over, you can see that the top, neater row, looks vaguely like back stitch, whereas the lower, more stretched out row looks like a random row of stab stitches.

6 Stretching the stitches becomes far more problematic as soon as you introduce curves, as you can see here that the bottom row has become quite jagged.

7 Stretching the stitches becomes far more problematic as soon as you introduce curves, as you can see here that the bottom row has become quite jagged.The main rule of split stitch in opus anglicanum is always to split something, so begin a new row by splitting the first stitch out the row it stands next to, and split into another row when you finish. Two rows that end in the same place can be split into a point, as here. You should never really see the end of a row of stitches in opus. There are exceptions, which I will mention when we come to them.

Materials

- Wool or linen canvas, approx. 45 × 30cm (18 × 12in)
- Crewel needle, size 22
- Crewel wool:
  - Weld yellow/bright yellow 553
  - Weld woad green mix/grass green 253
  - Madder rose/coral 861
  - Brown/red fawn 305
  - Madder red/coral 865
  - Madder orange/coral 863
  - Deep indigo blue/sky blue 568
  - Compound black/charcoal 998
  - Undyed white/white 991
  - Exhaust madder/flesh tint 706

Direction of Laidwork Stitching

When placing the laidwork, direction really doesn't matter. Choose the direction that will fill the space most quickly – this will also give the best coverage, as demonstrated by these two roughly similar long rectangles.

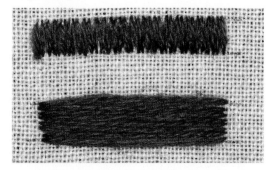

The top rectangle has been filled along the short edge. As a result, the filling has taken thirty-five stitches and the coverage along the long edge is somewhat ragged. The lower example has been filled along the long edge, using only eight stitches. Coverage along the long edge is complete, although the long laidwork threads will need to be nudged back into place with the couching. This direction is quicker and gives better coverage, and as this type of stitching is essentially intended to cover large areas as quickly as possible, longer stitches make more sense.

The Background

Begin with the yellow background; yellow being chosen to imitate the gold leaf that forms the background of many medieval manuscripts.

1 Work the background using weld yellow/bright yellow.

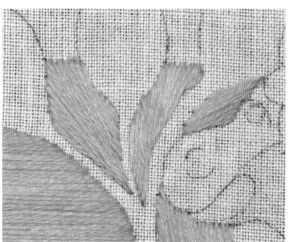

2 I've filled some areas using a flared technique. This is useful for filling in odd triangular spaces without doing too many tiny stitches, which can make the pointy bits look messy and uneven.

Flared Laidwork Stitch

I've filled some areas with a flared technique. It can be hard to get to grips with this little refinement at first, but it's worth persisting because it can fill awkward spaces much more elegantly.

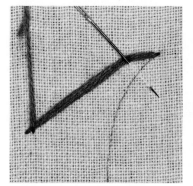

To work this flared technique, take the first long stitch right into the pointy bit. When you bring the second stitch in, tuck it under the first, rather than bringing it down at the side of the slope. The distance at which you need to tuck it under will vary from piece to piece – somewhere between 10 and 20 percent of the distance is about right.

This two-tone version clearly demonstrates how the flared technique works.

When it is all done in the same colour, the shape becomes very smooth at the edges.

From the back, you can see that at the wide end of the triangle the stitches are spaced normally, but at the narrow end they overlap a little.

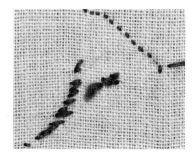

3 If you look closely, you can see some of my yellow filling is horizontal, some is vertical and there's even one bit that's diagonal, but when you step back your eyes blur it into one big mass of yellow. When the rest of the details are put into place, the changes in direction will be even less obvious. There are occasions when the direction of the laidwork is important, but these are the exception rather than the rule. This is a historically accurate approach.

The Border

Along the narrow bands of the outer border, it would be tedious to work part of the green stripe in short stitches and part in long stitches, and the short edges would be prone to messiness. Instead, we will follow the principle of taking the laziest line by mitring the corners of the green stitching so we can use the longest stitches possible.

4 Mitre the corners of the green stitching, using the longest stitches possible.

Mitring the Corners

Mitring the corners is done by overlapping the stitches at the corners. I've demonstrated this in three different colours here.

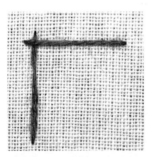  

Placing a couching bar directly over the join covers it completely, making the corner seamless.

Each corner forms a small cross, sticking out maybe 3–4mm (⅛in) at most. It looks a little clumsy at first, but each subsequent layer covers the one before, giving a lovely sharp corner. Only the final layer needs to be done with neat matching edges.

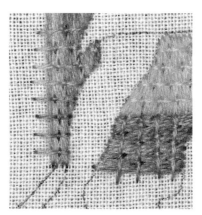

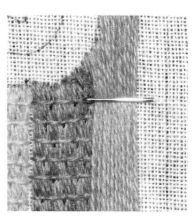

5 The normal way of couching laidwork creates two quite separate areas of colour, usually with a small gap that we can later cover with an outline. On the layered bands of outline, we want a seamless blend between the colours as there will be no outline to cover any gaps.

6 Instead of pulling the sides of the long green threads into line with the couching bars by couching right at the edge of the green, in this case we throw the couching bar out a few millimetres into the space to be covered by the next colour. Like the mitred corners, this can look at little spidery at first, but it eventually gives a much neater result.

7 Put the next layer of laidwork – in this case madder rose/coral – in place, mitring the corners as before. Then bring the madder rose couching bars out by splitting them out of the previous row of green ones to create a continuous line. This allows the two colours to butt up against each other seamlessly.

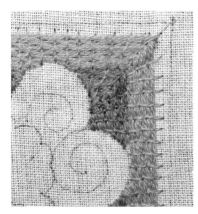

8 We want the madder rose to blend just as seamlessly with the outer row of brown that will follow, so as well as splitting out of the green couching bars, you will want to throw the madder rose bars out a little, as you did with the green ones. The only place you should need to add a discrete extra bar or two is at the corners, where the bars radiate out.

9 Add the outer brown/red fawn segment, joining it on and blending it in the same way. You don't need to throw the couching bars out because the brown outer edge is also the outer edge of the border.

The Bonacon, Tree and Knights

The Bonacon in the original manuscript doesn't have quite such a cheesy grin, but there's always room for improvement when adapting an image for embroidery. The colours used for the knights are a lovely example of how the colours of medieval art create a visual rhythm, which makes the most of our limited palette of colour.

The tree buds are quite art-nouveau looking, and in this case the white detailing makes them look springlike. You could make up your own frond pattern, or simply outline an enormous oak leaf inside each blue blob, which would look perfectly medieval. Medieval trees are usually extremely abstract.

10 Fill the main panel of the Bonacon's body in madder red/coral.

Varying the Flared Laidwork Stitch

The tail is an awkward shape to fill, but once you get the hang of the flared laidwork stitch, you can use a variation to curl around the curves of the tail, as demonstrated here in two colours.

Fill the tail by varying the flared laidwork stitch to curl around the curves.

11 Use madder orange/coral to fill his neck and little wig. There's no need to fill them as separate areas; it's quicker to sew them as a single blob and add definition when we come to outline. Fill the Bonacon's rear legs and the legs and helmet of the far-left knight at the same time.

12 Fill and couch the shield in weld woad green mix/grass green. When filling the tree trunk with green, you will need to practise those curves a little. Couch the trunk diagonally in contrasting brown/red fawn to create a stylised bark effect.

13 Use deep indigo blue/sky blue for the Bonacon's hooves, the tips of the spear and axe, the buds upon the tree, and the legs and helmet of the other knight.

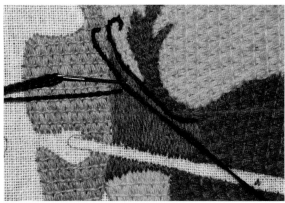

14 Use brown/red fawn to do the laidwork on the toxic fart cloud. Normally it would be easier to fill this area horizontally and use some flaring out to fill the space, however in this case we're going to fill the brown in vertically. This will allow for some decorative couching to create that tasteful splatter effect across the shield.

15 You'll need two needles for this part: one with a double thread and another with a single. Use the double to create the bar and couch it with the single. Instead of taking the bar across, plunging it down and then couching it, allow that bar to curve and curl as you couch it, plunging it once you're happy with the shape you've created.

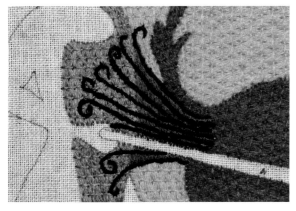

16 Don't try and be too rigid and symmetrical; it's meant to look like shit – literally!

17 The final bit of plain couching is to use some of the same madder rose/coral we used in the border for the spear, and a little bit of brown/red fawn for the axe handle and the base of the tree.

18 Use trellis couching to give the texture of chainmail armour. The far-left knight gets deep indigo blue/sky blue laidwork, compound black/charcoal trellis and madder rose/coral couching points. The poor chap holding the shield gets madder orange/coral laidwork, deep indigo blue/sky blue trellis and undyed white couching points.

19 I'm a terrible miser with thread when it comes from dyeing it myself, so I used a leftover scrap of compound black/charcoal from the trellis to outline the bull's eyes and nostrils using split stitch. The final bit of laid and couched work is a tiny bit of undyed white for his cheesy grin (like most serial farters, he's pleased with his endeavours). As with the fart cloud, the shape of his teeth would be easier to fill horizontally, but we're going to couch vertically again to create another special effect.

Trellis Couching

Trellis couching is used from time to time to add texture in medieval embroidery. Until the fifteenth century it was rarely used as a main filling stitch because it isn't quite as stable as regular laid and couched work. However, small areas of it sometimes turn up for texture, usually with a contrasting coloured couching stitch, and that's how we're going to use it today.

You can couch either once, horizontally or vertically, or do both and couch with a small crossed stitch. I find the crossed stitch can look a bit clunky, so I tend to go for a single vertical couching stitch.

I would advise filling in a systematic fashion by following one diagonal up and down, because if you dot around you might find you miss one, and you know you won't notice until you've finished and mounted the piece, wrapped it up, given it to your dad for Christmas. He'll already have proudly hung it in the downstairs loo, where it will forever taunt you every time you take a pee at your parents' house. We all know this to be a universal truth.

Do your laidwork area just as you would with ordinary laid and couched work, but in this case instead of laying down a single bar and then immediately stabilizing it, we're going to lay all the bars down at once. And instead of making them perpendicular to the laid stitches we'll do them at a 45-degree angle. It can be a bit tricky to get the angles consistent at first, so it can help to hold the thread in place and move it around until you get the angle right. The first bar you lay down will dictate where you put the rest, so it's often best to start in the middle of the area to get a clean view, then work out to either side.

Repeat the process in the opposite direction to create a neat grid. This second layer is often much easier to lay accurately because you can use the first set as a guide (as long as they're reasonably neat to begin with).

The reason we need to lay the bars at once is because we're then going to couch them at the intersections. If things have gone at little awry you can nudge the grid back into place a little with the couching.

20 Couch the white laidwork with a single thread of black along the line of the teeth, then add some short single stitches for definition.

21 Use a single strand of black split stitch to outline the deep-red parts of the Bonacon's body and hooves, taking care to extend the outline into a point to exaggerate the jagged edges of his tail. Outline the shield and the knights' helmets, as well as creating some panels on the helmets. You might as well also do the outlines of knights' eyes and noses while you have the black thread in play.

22 Use a single strand of weld woad green mix/grass green to outline the spear shaft, axe handle and buds on the tree.

23 The only madder orange/coral outline is used for the knight with the blue legs. The knight with the orange legs gets a deep indigo blue/sky blue outline, as does the tree trunk.

24 Use another single strand of brown/red fawn split stitch to outline the Bonacon's rear legs.

25 For the Bonacon's mane and wig, use two strands of brown/red fawn couched with one strand to create swirls of couched outline. You don't need to copy my curls exactly, just create a nice organic swirly pattern (think Gustav Klimt), but it helps if the swirls are joined together by splitting each new swirl out from the edge of a previous one.

26 Depict both the knights' and Bonacon's faces with tightly packed split stitch done in a single strand of exhaust madder/flesh wool (it's the same principle as the opus anglicanum we'll look at in Chapter 6, but it's not opus as we're using wool). You could use a chunky filament silk for a textural contrast if you have some. It's best to do the knights first, because they aren't the real stars of the show, so any newbie mistakes will be less disastrous. (Also because your average knight was probably a bit battle-scarred anyway.)

   Start by making arches to depict the swell of their cheeks – if their faces were shown in full these would be spirals, but their faces are hidden under their chainmail.

27 Work along the brow and, where possible, down the nose. Repeat this line until the area is filled. The shape of the face is expressed not with different colours but with the shape and direction of stitch.

28 Fill the under brow. The important thing here is to pack the stitches really close together and to always split something: split into and out of the previous rows to blend the stitches into one slab of flesh.

29 Now you have two options: you can either fill the upper lip in a solid block of apricot to depict flesh, or you can pick two contrasting colours and work paired stripes of stitches to create a truly ridiculous moustache (bonus points if you can curl it into the full handlebar soup strainer).

30 Before starting on the Bonacon's face, it's best to take care of his horns. These are done with the same trailed couching technique we used for the fart lines and wig, but this time the double strand of brown/red fawn is couched with a double strand of deep indigo blue/sky blue. I've taken more care in lining up the couching points into diagonal stripes to give his horns smart little ridges.

33 Take a single strand of madder red/coral and follow the line of brown down around his muzzle, extending it out from behind the eye into a spiral for his cheek. Notice how closely packed the stitches are so that no canvas shows through, and take care to shorten your stitches where necessary to account for the tight curves.

31 Take a single row of brown/ red fawn split stitch to outline the Bonacon's eyes, working a lovely swirly curve down from his top eye, along his upper muzzle and then outlining his cheesy grin. Outline his nostrils.

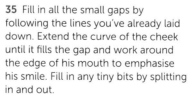

34 Continue the cheek spiral inwards until it is completely filled, then follow the same curving line out and down until the two sides meet between his eyes. This will leave a small area to be filled in on the nose, working around the nostrils. As long as you remember to split in and out of the previous rows (as in Step 28), his face will look like a nice unified piece of fur, and the shape of your stitches will express the shape of his face.

35 Fill in all the small gaps by following the lines you've already laid down. Extend the curve of the cheek until it fills the gap and work around the edge of his mouth to emphasise his smile. Fill in any tiny bits by splitting in and out.

32 Use white to highlight his eyes, nostrils and mouth.

Alternative Flaring Technique

You can use a similar flaring-out technique to the flared laidwork stitch that we used to bend the laid and couched work in split stitch to fill awkward curved areas. I've shown it here in two colours.

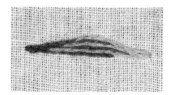

Simply work a row of stitches about two-thirds of the way along your shape, then switch across the back to split out of the same row and work along on top of it. Layers of stitches will build up in the middle to swell out the shape.

Finishing Touches

The final stage is to add some single lines of white split stitch in imitation of those seen in the original manuscript – these bring the whole thing to life. The wiggly white border pattern unifies the different coloured lines in the border, and it isn't nearly as difficult as it looks to work freehand.

36 Some undyed white lines, like the highlights on the Bonacon's hooves, are just little dashes of light. Others emphasise curves, like the lines on his body and tail.

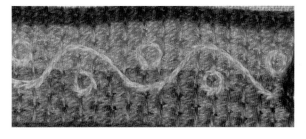

37 For the wiggly border, aim the apex of each curve for the middle of the green and madder rose band to keep the depth even. You can keep the length of each curve even by doing three stitches up, one across and three down. An alternate method is to work around the tip of your finger, to give a curve of about the right size.

Simply trace the curve with your needle when you need it to duck behind a leg or a head so that you can judge the correct exit point. Notice that the edge of each little circle touches the join between the two colours – you can ensure this by starting there. Do a couple of practice circles at the edge of the canvas: use eight to ten small stitches for each circle and they will stay roughly the same size.

38 The unfurling tree buds in the original manuscript are all slightly different, so I've used the same method to bring the white out from the branches to unify the elements.

CHAPTER 4

CONVENT STITCH

There is more than one illustration of the Brides of Christ harvesting ripe phalli from various bushes and trees lurking in the margins of medieval manuscripts, and obviously there's also more than one theory about their meaning.

One theory is that they are allegories of chastity, despite appearances. Another is that medieval folks genuinely believed that witches not only existed, but that they could also- and often did – physically steal men's penises. These purloined todgers were then secreted in oak trees (which have been associated with magic since the days of the Druids, although I must admit I first learned this fact from Getafix in *Asterix the Gaul* – a very educational series of books). But all was not lost, since virtuous maidens could retrieve them, hence the images.

I did read one folktale whereby a man whose pecker had been thus purloined made a bargain with a witch to get it back. After he'd held up his end of the bargain, she pointed to her oak tree and told him to help himself. Obviously, he came back with the biggest one he could find, only for the witch to tut at him and point out that that particular willy belonged to the local priest. I imagine witches do an awful lot of tutting.

It is up to you which version of the meaning you believe, but I suspect that to the medieval mind, both were equally true because tales and images can always have more than one meaning.

CONVENT STITCH METHOD

It feels as though convent stitch is just a different version of laid and couched work that evolved from the more conventional method (convent stitch comes along in around the thirteenth century, whereas laid and couched work had been around since before the Norman Conquest).

Unlike laid and couched work, where stitch direction is generally unimportant, this stitch tends to be worked in a uniform direction, generally perpendicular to the image. It's best to use a very long double strand for convent stitch, especially on the larger areas of the design, because otherwise you'll spend more time finishing and beginning strands than you will actually stitching. I'm using a contrasting colour for demonstration purposes, but the design couches in the same colour as the bar.

The harvest is bountiful this year!

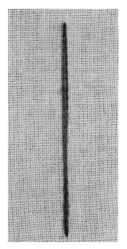  

1 Using two strands of wool, lay down a long bar over the area of design to be filled – so far, exactly the same as laid and couched work.

2 Simply couch back up the bar using the same double thread to create a sort of barber's pole/candy twist effect. This is really just like laid and couched work without the initial laid step, using the second step of couched bars and packing them tightly together.

3 Work another bar close to the side of it, repeating until the shape is filled. I find that to get good coverage and avoid gaps, it is best to nibble into the previous bar a little with the couching stitch.

CONVENT STITCH PROJECTS

Penis-Picking Nuns

I've previously completed a version of this legend featuring only one nun in laid and couched work. This time, I've reproduced the image where she's brought along one of her sisters for moral support. (Or maybe just so they can carry more willies – who knows?) For the sake of change, I've done this version in convent stitch, which was widely used in Germany and the Low Countries, most notably for the large hanging known as the Malterer embroidery, which depicts multiple tales of women getting the better of men.

There is more than one medieval image of nuns harvesting ripe todgers off various forms of shrubbery.

I've made this image quite large because convent stitch makes lovely cushions. I have adapted the surround from that of the Malterer embroidery, replacing the lilies with a small flower that looks remarkably like a penis. Of course, the design would work equally well in laid and couched work. I made the nuns blue because I grew up in the 1970s when Blue Nun Liebfraumilch was all the rage with Mum and Dad, and who can resist a good pun? And I added rabbits, just because.

Colour map for stitched filling.

Materials

- Wool or linen canvas, approx. 45cm (18in) square
- Crewel needle, size 18
- Crewel wool:
    - Weld yellow/bright yellow 553
    - Mid cochineal pink
    - Exhaust madder/flesh tint 706
    - Pale brown/chocolate 182
    - First madder red/coral 866
    - Undyed white/white 991
    - Woad blue/bright china blue 746
    - Oak grey/putty groundings 983

Colour map for outlines.

Penis-picking nuns template. Enlarge by 200%. Finished size 45cm (18in) square.

Getting Started and Stitching the Framework

Because this stitch is worked vertically to the image, I prefer to work away from my body as I find it helps me pack the stitches better. It's worth doing a few trial patches to work out your own preferred direction, as it may be different. I've set up my frame so that the image lies on its side to make stitching easier.

The border is a nice big stretch to get the hang of things. If you make the odd mistake in the border, it won't be the end of the world because the eye is drawn to the central image first. Only someone really picky is going to notice a mistake here.

1 Transfer the design to your canvas.

2 Begin by working the weld yellow/bright yellow border along one side of the image. Because of the linear, directional quality of this stitch, the lower border will be made from much smaller stitches, which are a bit fiddlier because you need to keep the edges straight (ish – you can cover minor wobbles with the outlines). It helps if you get the design dead square to the canvas. It doesn't matter which side you do next, just continue working out from wherever you end up.

Joining on a New Thread

You may find your thread runs out before you finish the row, especially along the very long sides of the border. It won't make any difference if this happens along the couching part, but if you find the thread isn't quite long enough for the first step, you can join a new thread on in much the same way that you would for laid and couched work:

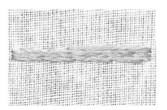

Simply stop the thread and finish it halfway along the line...

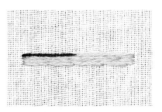

... and then pick up the long stitch by splitting it with the new thread before couching it down as usual. (I've used a contrasting colour for visibility.)

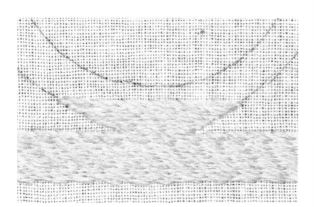

3 You will need to start the edge of the lobed quatrefoil as a new row and work out to either side separately.

4 The border takes a bit longer than you think it would because it's actually quite a big area spread thinly, but once it's in place you have a framework for the design.

Stitching in One Direction

Consistency is more important with convent stitch than with laid and couched work. Remember to always do your couching stitch in the same direction, either from top to bottom or bottom to top (or left to right or right to left if you prefer to work vertically). The direction doesn't matter, so long as it is consistent. One stitch in the wrong direction will stick out like a sore thumb.

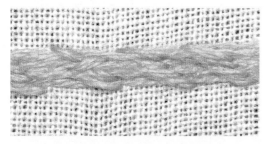

It's most important to pay attention to stitching in the same direction at the beginning, when picking the project up after a long break, or if, like me, you flip your frame to work from the opposite direction. In time, though, you will build up a rhythm and no longer need to think about it.

The Willies

I'm going to sew the willies in a mixture of pink and brown flesh tones (mainly because I am so utterly childish that I find the phrase 'mixed willies' extremely amusing), but I will unify the two by working all the foreskins in the same colour.

Medieval embroidery tends to work with a very limited colour palette, but it ends up creating a harmonious image, so I'm also filling the bunny's inner ear in the same pink.

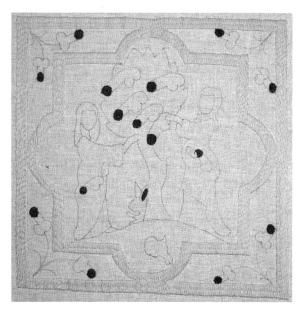

5 Start by filling in the foreskins and the bunny's ear in mid cochineal pink.

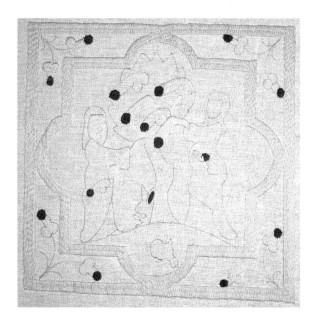

6 This limited colour panel enforces a kind of rhythm onto the image because colours must alternate. Here I've done the flowers in opposite corners in exhaust madder/ flesh tint, and the pink nun will have a pale brown/ chocolate willy gathered into her skirt, and vice versa. The phalluses on the tree are done in both colours, and I've tried to alternate them too.

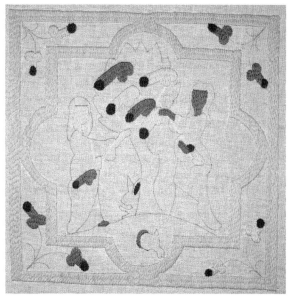

7 I've filled in the alternating cocks in pale brown/ chocolate, as well as the other nun's face and hands. I've also added pale brown/chocolate to make the shadow in the rabbit hole. You might be tempted to use a different shade of brown here, but I would urge you not to for two reasons. Firstly, the more colours you use, the less medieval the work will look. And secondly, a new colour used for just one small area will stand out and draw the eye too much.

The Tree, Grass, Stems and Border

Work in from the edges one colour at a time – green is next. The directional curve of the flower stems makes the stitch pretty similar to the trailed couching used for the Bonacon's fart cloud in Chapter 3.

Satin Stitch

You will start to find that some of the narrower spans of stitching become just too small to do a full couching stitch. Once you get down to about 5mm (¼in) or less, it's perfectly acceptable to make small satin stitches. Although satin stitch is not a medieval stitch as such (we still use it in the twenty-first century), it's used in all kinds of odd corners of medieval embroidery when the gap to be filled is simply too tiny to justify a full stitch.

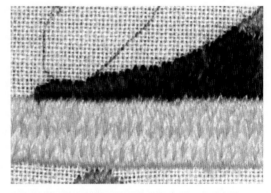

Filling the gaps in the grass with small satin stitches.

8 Use green for the tree, grass and flower stems.

9 The flower stems are so narrow, they wouldn't work well in the usual straight up and down style of convent stitch. Therefore, these are worked with a directional curve.

10 Use first madder red/coral to fill the border and tree trunk.

The Nuns, Bunnies and Background

The nuns' underdresses and veils could be worked in white, but because I plan to work the background in white I've made the visual distinction of using a very pale oak grey/putty groundings for these.

11 Use woad blue/bright china blue for the nuns' habits and bunnies.

12 Work the nuns' underdresses and veils in oak grey/ putty groundings.

13 Fill the remaining background in undyed white.

Outlining Stitches

You can use either stem or split stitch (*see* Chapters 2 and 3 for instructions) for the outlines. I tend to use a combination of the two because I find that stem stitch works better for some parts (especially the outside parts), whereas split stitch is better for small details like the faces or when you're drawing straight over a block of colour, like the dresses.

A single thread is used for all of the outline stitches, whether you use stem or split. It's best to use a much shorter length than you would for the filling stitch as the thread is placed under more stress by the smaller stitches.

Don't be intimidated by the element of freehand drawing when outlining. The figures are very cartoony and you don't have to place the lines exactly. (Look up the original images and you will see that the drawing is spectacularly bad, so you really can't do any worse!)

14 I used stem stitch in woad blue/bright china blue to outline the yellow border. Notice that I've drawn a line where the lobed quatrefoil in the middle meets the square border.

Stitch blue lines on the tree trunk for the bark. Don't be intimidated by placing this too exactly; it's bark, so it's meant to look organic.

15 Outline the green stems on the plants in weld yellow/bright yellow, working over the green to add extra definition to the leaves.

Stitching Fingers

When defining the fingers, it is better to outline just the sides of the hand, rather than the whole thing, as you can see from these two examples:

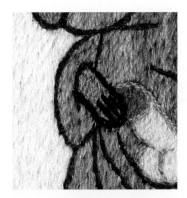

Here I outlined the hand first before adding definition lines for the fingers. It looks a bit clunky.

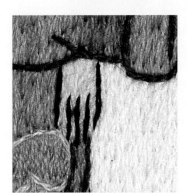

Whereas here I only outlined the sides of the hand before adding the finger lines. This gives a much better-looking result.

16 Use pale brown/chocolate to outline the pink willies, making sure to add some definition to the testicles.

17 Outline the brown willies in flesh pink. Use a tiny bit of the same colour to outline the inner ear of the cheeky bunny.

18 Use first madder red/coral to outline and define the folds in the nuns' habits. Make sure to add a swoop of fabric under the collected phalluses so it looks like they're holding them in their skirts.

Add some leaves to the tree – these should look organic, so don't feel you have to copy my placement exactly. I find it's best to define the leaves at the edges and then work inwards.

The bunnies should also be outlined in red.

19 I always use black sparingly as it can overpower an image. Here I'm using it to outline and define the hands and faces, add pleats (again, random is good) to the underskirts, and give the bunny an eye.

Outlining Faces

Black is also used to define the nuns' faces. This isn't nearly as scary to work as you'd think. It's really a very simple, cartoony sort of face and very easy to do.

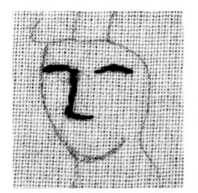

Once you've outlined the face and defined the chin, start by the outer edge of the left eyebrow, work across in a very slight curve until you're about one-third of the way across the brow, then go down and around the tip of the nose. Then work the other brow independently. You can use your couching bars as a gauge to make sure they are level.

Work the upper eyelashes as a straight line, level with the brow. The left-hand eye should 'tuck' under the nose line.

Make three or four short vertical satin stitches for the pupil.

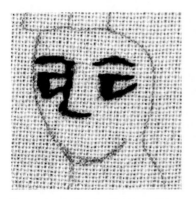

Sew a simple line for the lower lid.

The mouth is another simple line, two or three stitches in length.

Finishing Touches

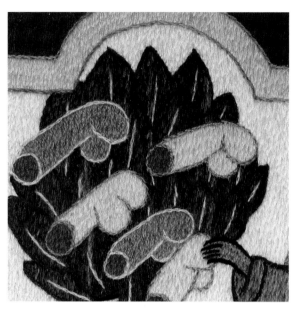

19 Use a tiny splash of undyed white for the bunny's tail and tummy.

20 And if you want to, you can add some yellow veins to the leaves on the tree.

21 And we're finished!

Phyllis

Giddy-up!

Convent stitch is such a simple technique that there was no justification on the bounds of expanding it to include a second project. So instead I offer a pattern based upon the Malterer hanging – the piece whose border I plundered for the Penis-Picking Nuns. I include it because it's slightly pervy, and it's a piece I often use as a demo because it has the narrative element of medieval art as a strong ingredient.

The story of Aristotle and Phyllis is one of four tales included in the original hanging, and they all share the common theme of women getting the better of men. I've read some very academic readings of the piece that say, 'Ah, but it shows the power of love, and men will do anything for love', and others that counter, 'Nonsense, this piece was displayed in a nunnery, and it is there to show the nuns that they were better off in the cloister away from all of that silly nonsense!' While there may be some truth in both of these interpretations, I think they forget that medieval people had a sense of humour – and a decidedly bawdy one at that. This is the tale of a pretty girl getting the better of a pompous old fart, something we snigger at today and which our ancestors sniggered at 500 years ago too.

There are many adaptations of the tale, so I'll tell you the version I tell to those who come to chat to me while I'm stitching my interpretation of this. If you've studied Ancient Greece at school, you will have heard of the philosopher Aristotle. Many people don't realise that Aristotle was tutor to a young man called Alexander the Great, but this was before he was all that great – back when he was simply Prince Alexander of Macedon.

One day, Alexander was staring out the window, instead of staring at his books, at a pretty young lady called Phyllis who was out in the garden. Aristotle said to him, 'You should break up with your girlfriend at once, young man. You are a prince, you have work to do, and you do not have time for girlfriends.'

So Alexander, being a dutiful and conscientious young man, leaned out of the window and said, 'Sorry, pet, my teacher says I'm not allowed a girlfriend, ok? Thanks. Bye.'

Phyllis was furious. She didn't love Alexander or anything soppy like that, she simply wanted to marry him. Now before you brand our Phyllis a gold-digger, bear in mind that there were no jobs for girls back then. A young lady's career was the man she married. Phyllis was just an ambitious, career-minded young woman. She decided to get her own back on Aristotle, and she did it in the girliest way possible. She put on her best frock, did her hair and paraded up and down outside Aristotle's study window, batting her eyelashes for all she was worth, until very soon it was the teacher who was hanging out of the window, begging Phyllis for a quick kiss.

'Eww!' says she, 'I'm not snogging you! Trouble with you philosophers is you're too busy thinking all the time to take a bath now and then. You smell like an old goat, you do!'

Aristotle continued to beg, whine and wheedle in a most undignified fashion, swearing he'd do anything for just one kiss, until Phyllis finally said, 'Well, my pony went lame last week and I haven't been able to go riding. You know I'm such a keen equestrian. If you let me ride you like a pony, I always kiss my pony on the nose when I get off.'

Outline colour map.

Full colour map.

Materials

- Linen or wool canvas, 41cm (16in) square
- Crewel needle, size 22
- Crewel wool:
  - Weld yellow/bright yellow 555
  - Strong madder red/scarlet 503
  - Undyed white/white 991
  - Dark bottle green/Jacobean green 297
  - dark cornflower blue 465
  - Compound black/charcoal 998
  - mid blue 462
  - grey 962
  - tan 302
  - bright green 424

Template. Enlarge by 400%. Finished size 41cm (16in) square.

Aristotle was flustered, 'I can't do that! I'm important public figure – people will laugh at me!'

Phyllis shrugged, 'Well, you did say you'd do anything for a kiss. Besides, if you come out to the orchard first thing tomorrow morning, nobody will be watching.'

The next morning, thinking only of kisses, Aristotle scuttled out to the orchard. He bent down on all fours, put on the saddle and a bridle and let Phyllis ride him like a pony. (Side-saddle of course – she was a lady!) No sooner had she whipped his bottom into a nice swift canter, she called out, 'You can come out now!'

From behind trees and bushes came the ladies and gentlemen of the court, including Alexander, and when they saw this dignified gentleman being ridden like a pony, they didn't just giggle, they didn't just chuckle, they laughed so hard they nearly wet themselves!

So, you see, Aristotle wasn't the only one to learn an important lesson that day, Alexander and the rest of the court also learned that there's no fool like an old fool.

CHAPTER 5

GERMAN BRICK STITCH

Although a great deal of German counted work is used in a single pattern for purses and cushions, there are also large-scale pieces like the Hildesheim cope that use the simple geometric patterns and incorporate them into figurative scenes, and I find these much more exciting. The simplest of my German counted work projects is based around the wonderful Cerne Abbas Giant – an ancient chalk-cut figure from Dorset.

GERMAN BRICK STITCH METHOD

This is a really simple counted stitch, quite similar to modern needlepoint. Each stitch covers four vertical threads, and stitches four threads long are arranged brick fashion. Medieval embroidery consistently keeps as little thread as possible on the back of the work to conserve expensive threads, especially with techniques like this one that primarily use silk in period.

Counted patterns, like those we're going to use in the background, generally use whole stitches. However, with the Cerne Abbas Giant design, we're going to use brick stitch to colour in an outline. You have to use your judgement to fit the stitches around the design, which will often involve the use of partial stitches.

The giant.

Sheela-na-gig.

1 Stitch along four threads of the cloth at the front. Carry two down and one over to come out in a diagonal line.

2 Take the shortest step across the back so as to waste the least amount of thread here.

3 Vertical edges are pretty straightforward, but horizontal ones are trickier. You have a choice of using a half stitch to line up...

4 ...or a one-and-a-half/longer stitch.

GERMAN BRICK STITCH PROJECTS

The Cerne Abbas Giant

For our giant I've chosen a simple broad zigzag pattern in yellow and pink to represent the waving, ripe corn in golden harvest fields, which seemed quite fitting for a fertility symbol.

This design is stitched throughout using two strands of 30/2 silk, but like the other German brick stitch designs you could just as easily use any silks, wools or stranded cottons you have on hand. I would suggest doing a test patch to decide how many strands works best for each thread.

Materials

- Wool or linen evenweave 32-count canvas, approx. 30cm (12in) square
- Crewel needles, size 22 and 18 (for the white silk)
- Silk 30/2nm threads:
  - Green
  - Pink
  - Yellow
- White fluffy caterpillar 2.5/2nm silk, approx. 1m (39in)
- White silk thread for sewing

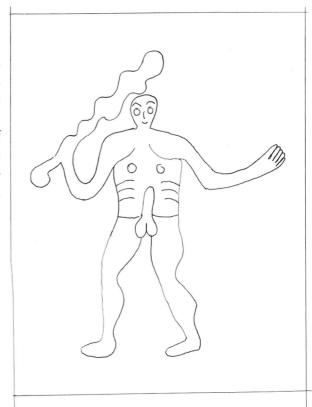

Template for the giant. Enlarge by 200%. Finished size 30cm (12in) square.

Transferring the Pattern

We're going to use brick stitch to colour in the areas, so counting the entire thing isn't necessary.

Filling in the Giant

It's best to start by just picking a place where you can work a line of stitches in a clear diagonal and work from there. I've chosen the giant's ankle based on the principle that I like to make my mistakes somewhere a bit less noticeable.

1 Transfer your design to the canvas using a permanent fabric marker.

2 Use two strands of 30/2 silk throughout. My silk is naturally dyed so it has small colour variations. Stitch a diagonal line in green from the shin to the ankle.

3 You can then fill out either side of your line, using partial stitches along the edges to follow the shape.

4 Remember to keep the stitches short at the back.

5 Coverage at the back is quite minimal, but should still follow the overall shape.

6 As you fill the body in green, take care to leave a narrow gap about two threads of the background canvas wide. This will accommodate the eventual placement of the fluffy caterpillar silk for the white lines.

Working the Zigzag Pattern

I'm not sure you really need a charted pattern for the zigzag background, but I'll provide one just in case. For those of you who, like me, struggle with charts, there are ten stitches to each side of the peak. I thought fewer stitches looked a bit weak and indistinct, but feel free to experiment.

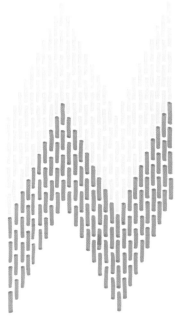

Simple zig zag pattern.

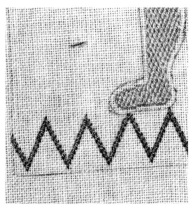

7 I started with the pink stripe, allowing its lower points to hit the bottom line of my background.

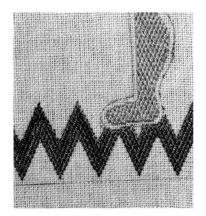

8 Work in blocks of four rows, remembering to leave a narrow gap around the figure for the eventual outline.

9 Fill the lower triangles with yellow and work a yellow block above the pink one.

10 As long as you're consistent with the pattern, it should match up once you get to the top of his head (although I always find that bit quite nerve-racking).

Adding the Chalk Lines

The final step is to stitch the fluffy caterpillar silk down into the chalk lines. Use a single strand of the fluffy silk couched with a single strand of white sewing silk (white 30/2 is fine, but any sewing-weight white thread will do).

This is the same basic technique as the bars on the laid and couched work in Chapter 3, such as the couched outlines used for the Bonacon. You will need the big crewel needle to ease the fluffy silk through the fabric at each end, and the smaller crewel needle to stitch it down.

Don't put your couching stitches too close together: 4mm (⅛in) is about right – you want the silk to be able to 'floof' out a bit.

11 Start with the internal details, where the ends will be covered by the outline (face, fingers, ribs and nipples). His nipples are quite tricky as they need to be worked in a teeny tiny spiral.

12 Work around his wibbly wobbly club next. Make sure to leave the line between the club and his hand as that belongs to the outline of his body.

Bring your silk out right underneath his testicles for the next step – this makes an ideal starting point as it's the only real break in the outline of the body.

13 Work all the way around the outline of his body.

14 Save his willy for last. He's obviously quite pleased with it and wants everyone to see it. Working it last will make it stand proud, so to speak.

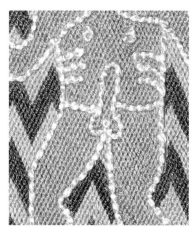

15 Jolly little chap, isn't he?

Sheela-na-gig

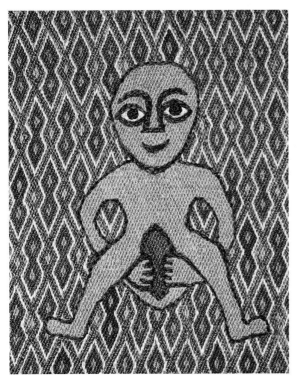

The finished Sheela.

Sheela-na-gig template. Enlarge by 200%. Finished size 30cm (12in) square.

Sheela-na-gigs are mostly found on Romanesque churches. Whether they are fertility figures, a female equivalent of the green man or simply grotesques is a matter hotly debated, but personally I favour the fertility figure theory on the basis that some of them have had their clitorises polished over the centuries by the rubbing of many fingers that perhaps hoped for a blessing. I based my Sheela on the one from Kilpeck church in Herefordshire, perhaps the most well-known of them all.

I've provided a chart for the background pattern used here, which is from the Hildesheim cope. I chose this particular pattern because it very much echoes the shape of the main area that draws one's eye, and the colour was chosen on the same basis.

I admit it makes a fantastic social media shot to work all the bits of one colour and then fill in the rest around it. If you can follow a chart, then do so. I can't follow counted charts – I'm hopeless at it, and as soon as I'm expected to count stitches I get completely bamboozled. So, for the sake of those of you who share my impediment, I'm going to talk you through my approach to a counted work pattern, which is to break it down into shapes and think about the shapes rather than the numbers.

Materials

- Wool or linen evenweave 32-count canvas, 30cm (12in) square
- Crewel needle, size 22
- Silk 30/2nm threads:
  - Pink
  - Yellow
  - White
  - Blue
  - Green
  - Dark brown

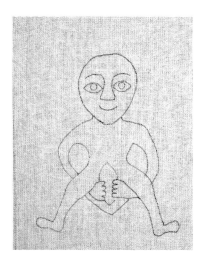

Chart for the background design.

Filling in the Figure

When filling the figure in, her fingers are a bit tricky because they're so tiny. This is one of those cases where a tiny bit of satin stitch is perfectly acceptable.

1 Transfer your design to the canvas using a permanent fabric marker.

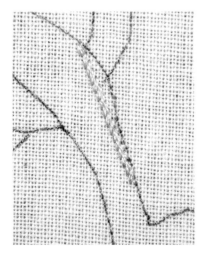

2 Choose a nice long line to start your row of diagonal stitching. I chose her leg.

3 Fill the figure in yellow, leaving gaps for her face and the lines that delineate the figure.

4 Fill her vagina in pink, and then it's time to move on to the geometrical bit.

The Background

If you think about it in terms of shape, the dominant shape here is the diamond.

The Pink Diamonds

Your pink diamond shapes are going to be six stitches long along the outer edge and two stitches wide. The holes should be two stitches tall. (Basically, the smallest diamond you can possibly make in this technique is a negative with the pink worked around it.) Alternatively, you could work the tiny green diamond first then work the pink around that, but I prefer to leave spaces for the teensy diamonds and do them all at once.

The Blue Diamonds

The blue is another set of diamonds overlaid with more diamond shapes. Due to my inability to count stitches, I find it easier to work one of two diamonds at a time, filling in all of the colours as I go along. I'm afraid that perfect Instagram shot of the entire piece covered in naked blue diamonds will forever elude me. Make sure to leave a narrow gap all around the figure so you can fit an outline later.

5 Choose a random space in the middle of the background where you can work your first shape without bumping into anything else. Work a diamond with a hole in the middle. Work a second diamond as though the points overlap. You now have two overlapping diamonds that contain two tiny negative diamond shapes.

6 Work a single row of white around the outside of the pink diamonds.

Making Mistakes

You can see here that I accidentally filled a couple of my small diamonds. I hate unpicking so I'm just going to stitch over the mistakes later. Silk will allow you to stitch over your mistakes, but cotton won't (cotton will become lumpy). So if you chose to work in cotton you'll have to pick things out.

I wasn't paying enough attention to the negative spaces here.

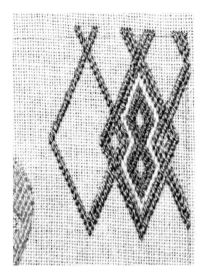

7 Work a double row of blue out from the point of the pink/white shape, but where the smaller diamonds overlap and the shape kinks in to the side. Keep going out until you reach the point where the blue rows coming from both points of the diamonds meet.

    The next blue diamond is worked out from where the pink/white shape kinks in to the side, and creates another tiny diamond in negative.

8 When you overlay another diamond you can see how it creates a negative space equivalent to the pink/white shape.

9 Once I've got a few blue diamonds worked out to the side of the original, not only can I fill in the pink and white to the side, but I can also use what I have to start working vertically.

The Yellow and Green Diamonds
The final step to complete the background is to fill in all of your tiny negative spaces.

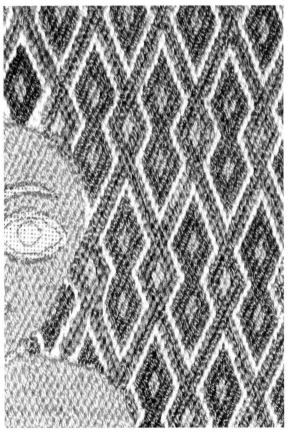

10 I've used green in the pink gaps and yellow in the blue ones.

Details and Outlines

Split stitch (*see* page 45) is better for the whites because it blends better. I left enough space for a double row of stitching on her face to echo the fairly rough carving of the original figure (plus I like the way it makes her look like she's wearing eyeliner). However, around the edge of the body I left a much narrower gap to accommodate only a single row of stitching.

11 Use dark brown split or stem stitches to work small spirals for the pupils of her eyes.

12 Add some white to fill in her eyes.

13 Work the outline of her facial features with a double row of brown split stitch.

14 Outline the body with a single row of brown split stitch.

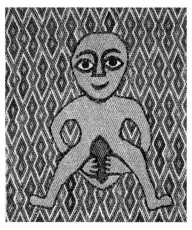

15 The finished Sheela.

Full Moon Over Cologne

This little charmer is based on a carving situated on the outside of Cologne City Hall. Seeing as he's German, it seems a natural choice to surround him with German brick stitch. There is a similar figure carved into one of the roof beams of Hereford Cathedral.

I've mixed things up a little here, and instead of filling the figure with more brick stitch, I've worked him in silk laid and couched work.

Full moon.

Full moon template. Enlarge by 200%. Finished size 30cm (12in) square.

Materials

- Wool or linen evenweave 32-count fabric, about 30cm (12in) square
- Crewel needle, size 22
  - Silk 30/2nm threads:
  - Pale pink
  - Dark pink
  - White
  - Pale brown
  - Dark brown
  - Russet
  - Green
  - Blue

Filling in the Figure

The laid and couched work in silk follows the same principles as the wool laid and couched work, but because the thread is thinner you need to scale down the spacing in proportion to the thread width, so the bars should be a maximum of 4mm (⅛in) apart. We'll fill in the main shapes and leave any detailing for later.

1 Mark the design onto the canvas using a permanent fabric marker.

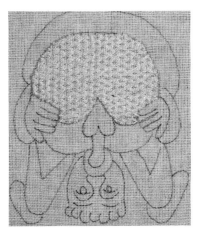

2 For all of the laid and couched work, use two strands of pale pink silk couched with one strand. Fill his enormous backside. Don't try to delineate separate buttocks at this stage; we can do that later.

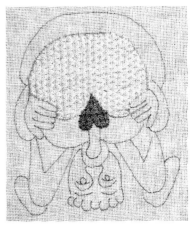

3 Fill his testicles with dark pink.

4 Work his white underwear as one large blob for now (and just be grateful that it's clean – things could always be worse!).

5 His hose (trousers in modern parlance, though these may be the separate legged kind that are more like stockings; it's hard to tell) are filled in pale brown.

6 Fill his shoes in dark brown.

The Brick Stitch Background

As with the Sheela-na-gig, you can follow the chart if you prefer, but I'm going to explain the design by shape for the hard of counting (me).

7 Start with a small russet diamond, six stitches per side on the outer edge with a two-stitch tall voided diamond in the centre.

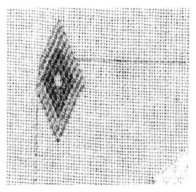

8 Surround the diamond with two rows of green.

The design chart.

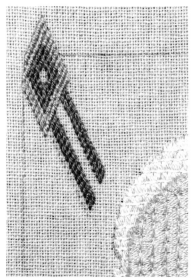

9 Two rows of russet stitch, each fourteen stitches long, extend out parallel to each edge of the diamond. It's as if the russet lines have jumped the green and extended out in the same direction. There should be space for two more stitches between these lines, and this space lines up with the voided diamond in the centre of the russet one.

10 These are then crossed by two more double lines. Each arm of the double hatch should be four stitches long, with a gap of two stitch spaces between, leaving another tiny voided diamond in the centre.

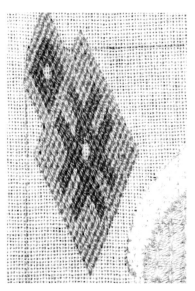

11 You can then work a double row of green around the hatching, extending the points out into a larger diamond and filling all but the central space.

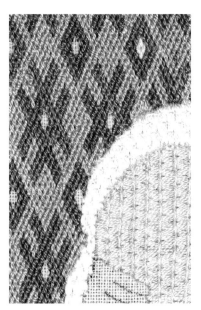

12 The next set of hatch marks line up against the side of this green triangle, and the next set of russet diamonds are parallel to the ends of the hatching.

13 By working methodically out from this first pattern, you can fill the entire background.

14 Lastly, fill the little voided diamonds with white, or a colour of your choice – you could go for two colours like I did with Sheela.

Alternate Brick Patterns for the Background

As well as the Hildesheim diamonds design used here, you can substitute the backgrounds with these alternative brick patterns.

Four-diamond Hildesheim

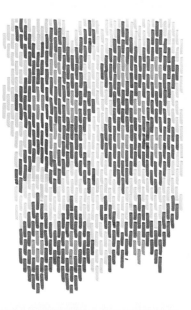

Four- and five-diamond Hildesheim

Outlining the Figure

Now that the background is in place, we can go back to outlining the figure. Leaving the outline until now means that we can cover the edges of the brick stitch as well, making things neater.

15 Use a single strand of blue split stitch to work the folds of his undies and shoes.

16 Use dark brown to outline the rest, including his face, hands and the curls of his hair. You can also put some hairs on his testicles at this point with just a few little stab stitches.

Working the Hands

Hands are really simple; just work out from the fingertips with one strand of pale pink split stitch (*see* page 45).

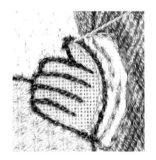

17 Work around the wrist and into the top of his thumb.

18 Continue until you fill up one finger, splitting the rows together at the tips of his fingers, and then allow the natural curve of the stitching to lead into the next finger.

19 If you find the curve too tight to stitch neatly at any point, you can split into the previous row.

20 Continue until the hands are completely full.

The Face and Hair

We'll use a single strand of split stitch to model his face in an almost opus anglicanum style. It won't be proper opus because it's the wrong kind of silk, but it's good practice.

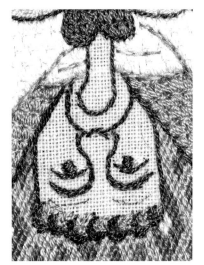

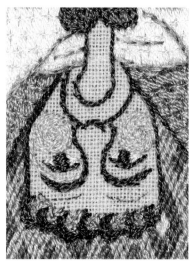

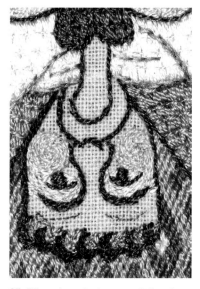

21 Fill in the curls with some pale brown and add a few touches of white to his eyes.

22 Start outlining his cheeks. They should be nice and round because of all the, erm… effort he's putting in! Fill all of the available space, making the edges of each circle touch the edge of his eye, nose, and the outline of his face, then work an inward spiral until each cheek is filled. Next, split out from the edge of the cheek and work a line under his brow and down to the corner of his eye.

23 Fill each under brow, splitting the beginning of each row of stitching out from a previous row, and splitting them all into the first row at his eye to make the skin flow as one piece of flesh.

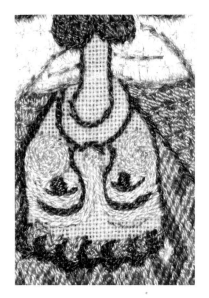

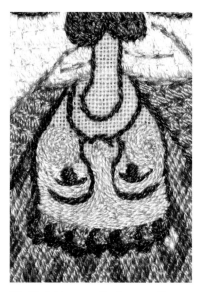

24 Split out from the dark brown outline on one side. Work over the brow and down around the tip of his nose before heading over the other brow and splitting back into the outline. You may need to add a small row to fill in either side of the eyebrow beforehand, just to level things out.

25 Fill right across the brow until you reach the hairline.

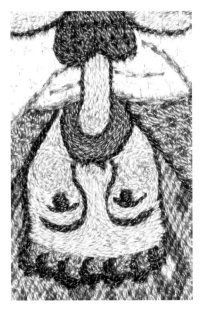

26 Split into and out of the previous rows of stitching to fill the sides of his nose and lower cheeks. Repeat for any other tiny gaps to finish the face, then work his lips in dark pink.

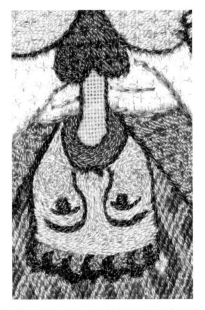

27 Work the shaft of his penis in the same pale pink colour as his face.

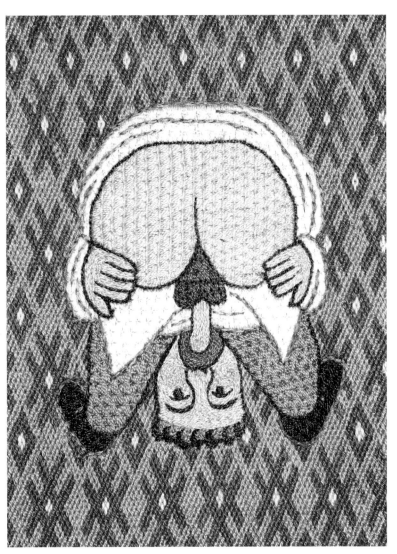

28 I hope you've enjoyed stitching him as much as he is enjoying his acrobatic little self. .

CHAPTER 6

OPUS ANGLICANUM

Opus anglicanum is recognised as one of the great art forms of the Middle Ages. Found in both the ecclesiastical context of copes and mitres, as well as the more secular context of almoner purses, it was prized and traded all over Europe for centuries, often in the form of diplomatic gifts. During the reformation unknown quantities of embroidery were destroyed to retrieve the precious metal content of the thread.

In theory opus anglicanum is simply a combination of split stitch (*see* page 45) and underside couching, but often practice is not as simple as theory. I would only define something as opus anglicanum if the split stitch is done with filament, also known as flat or reeled silk. These silks are untwisted, allowing the stitch to utilise the full shine of the silk fibre; use a different silk and the shine is gone, and the shine is a major element of opus. Instead of being an equal partner to the shimmer of gold, split stitch done in twisted silk or cotton just becomes a dowdy afterthought to the main event. Banks of shining stitches can be used to manipulate light, providing just as much glow as the goldwork when the correct silk is used. (Basic split stitch technique is covered in the Bonacon project in Chapter 3. Further tips for working split stitch as a filling can be found in my book *Opus Anglicanum* (Crowood, 2021).)

All medieval art has a certain cartoonish element, using narrative and symbolism to tell stories to a largely illiterate audience. Opus adds an almost manga-esque look with its emphasis on the eyes and hand gestures of the people depicted, because it's meant to be interpreted from afar. Hellmouth.

GOLDWORK: UNDERSIDE COUCHING METHOD

Underside couching is often seen as a very difficult stitch, but if you approach it properly it's really easy and satisfying. Underside couching is never used in the medieval period as an outlining stitch; it's always a filling stitch, so single rows aren't a thing.

It is important to understand the nature of the thread we're using here, because you need to work *with* the thread rather than against it. Passing thread is made from a cotton core with a thin spiral of metal wrapped around it. In medieval times, this would have been a horsehair in the earliest period, moving on to silk or linen later, both wrapped in either pure gold, silver or silver gilt.

Modern goldwork tends to secure the end of the thread as part of the finishing process, but underside couching needs the thread secure before beginning, so the first hurdle is getting the end of the thread through the canvas. If you try to push the end of the passing thread through the eye of a needle, you tend to shred the gold off it, so instead take a large-eyed crewel needle and push a loop of thread through the eye. Always leave the thread in the longest piece possible, especially when working to fill a large area. You only use a needle on the gold thread at the beginning and end of each stretch.

Anchor your linen well at the back of the canvas. The colour of the linen thread doesn't matter as you will never see it, but yellow is great for beginners because the occasional missed stitch will be disguised by its colour. What you're looking for in a linen thread is strength, and not all linens are equal on that count. The stuff I use is strong, so I can't snap it easily with my bare hands.

The one problem people tell me they have with this stitch, over and over again, is that they can't find the same hole to go back down through. So, the second secret of success in underside couching is to make that hole big enough to be able to find it again. Using a chunky needle is a good start because it makes a bigger hole. Don't worry about the size of the holes; they will get pushed back together as you pack your stitches.

It is rare to break the gold thread (I've never done it) because it shouldn't be under enough tension to break. However, the linen takes a lot of punishment and will break from time to time, mainly because it wears. Minimise the stress and wear on the linen thread by pulling on the area of thread close to the canvas, thereby moving the area of stress along the thread as you work. If you pull on the needle every time you couch the thread, not only will it break very quickly but you also won't have precise control of your couching. You will sometimes forget to wrap your linen around your gold – when you do this you are allowed to swear at it.

1 Preparation is the secret to your success here, and by preparation I mean getting your canvas tight. It should be tight enough that you can confidently set a full mug of tea down on top of your work without any worry. I quite like demonstrating this at classes while people squeak in horror (just make sure the bottom of your mug is nice and clean). In this case, I used a wine bottle.

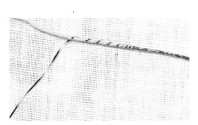

2 Our thread is cotton wrapped in gold-coloured plastic. As you can see, it unravels with alarming ease.

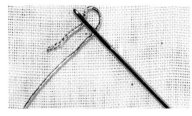

3 The same size 22 crewel needle we'll use for the stitching is great, but you may need to flatten the thread a little, either by squashing it with a pair of pliers or crushing it with your teeth.

4 Do not pull the thread all the way through the needle – this will shred it. You aren't going to be actively sewing with this thread; all you need to do is pull the end through the canvas. So just ease out the end of the loop. About 2cm (¾in) or so is enough to grip the needle for the single stitch that's needed here. It doesn't matter if the very tip of the thread is damaged because no one will ever see it.

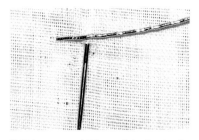

5 Take your gold through to the back of your canvas and anchor it firmly – you can use a waste knot if you prefer, or just slide it through the back of your previous stitching.

6 You only take the end through from the front, not the whole thread from the back. If you have your passing thread on a reel, leave it on the reel and pop it in a bag hanging from the frame, or catch it into the lacing of your frame to stop it rolling around.

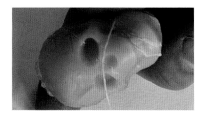

7 Now take the size 22 crewel needle and thread it with a well-waxed linen thread. Just run your thread a couple of times over a lump of beeswax. (It doesn't have to be skull-shaped, but it seemed appropriate for the Danse Macabre.)

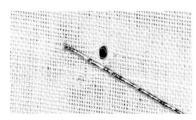

8 Bring the needle through the canvas, about 4mm (⅛in) from your starting point, but don't take it all the way through. Stop it halfway and give it a wiggle from side to side (against the grain, not up and down through the canvas). This will give you a big enough hole that you'll be able to find it again on the way down.

At this point, you will know whether or not your canvas is tight enough. If the hole appears after wiggling, the canvas is tight enough for underside couching. If the hole doesn't appear and the canvas moves around with the wiggling needle, then the canvas is too slack.

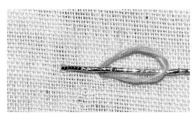

9 Loop the linen around the gold and head back down the hole.

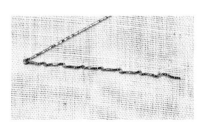

11 Do this repeatedly at 4–5mm (⅛in) intervals. Don't worry too much if your first row doesn't sit exactly straight; this is a filling stitch and packing the rows very tight together will iron out any initial wobbliness.

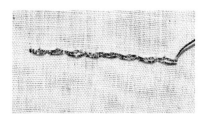

13 The brick arrangement of stitches is by far the most common one used in the medieval era, simply spacing the next row of couching points at intervals between the first.

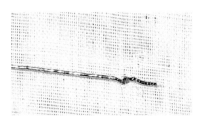

10 Use the linen to pull the gold down through the hole.

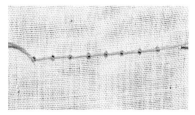

12 I'm not one to obsess about the back of the work being as perfect as the front, but knowing what the back of your stitch should look like often helps to understand how it works. In this case, you can see that all that shows of the gold at the back is a row of little nubs.

14 Build up layers of stitches by working back and forth. To get the stitches well packed together, you need to almost come up a little bit underneath the thread in the previous row, as the metal thread won't spread the same way that fibrous ones will.

Underside couching isn't done by leaving a fringe of loose gold threads at each end, as is customary in modern goldwork; firstly because this method messes with your tension, and secondly because although modern gold thread is relatively cheap, medieval ones were real gold and silver, so were far too expensive to waste in such a profligate fashion. Returning the end at each row wastes the minimum amount of thread; a common theme in all medieval embroidery techniques.

Troubleshooting

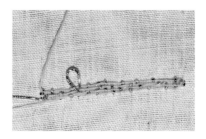

As you practise, you will be able to feel when the gold pulls through too much, but when you're learning it helps to check. You don't want big loops of gold like the one shown at the back, as they can work loose at any time and give you big loops on the front instead. Always check the back before you sign off on a piece.

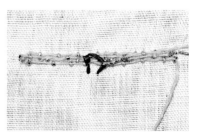

Any stray loops can be sewn down into the back of the linen threads, as I've shown here in a contrasting colour.

Opus Anglicanum Projects

Sid Snot

Sid is a variation on one of my favourite gurning demons from the *Luttrell Psalter*, with a diaper patterned border copied from those commonly found in fourteenth-century manuscripts. He is an example of using manuscripts as inspiration, rather than directly copying an extant piece. The diapering is tricky because it needs a certain accuracy in laying down the chequered bars, but it's quite rewarding once you get the hang of it.

Sid's face is worked in two colours, rather than the usual one seen in both opus anglicanum and manuscript illustrations. This is often used as an indication that the person is wicked or somehow dubious, but I think in this case he's just a very naughty boy!

Sid is a little charmer!

Sid Snot template. Enlarge by 200%.
Finished size 20cm (8in) square.

Materials

- Double-layered ramie or linen canvas, roughly 90 count, 20cm (8in) square
- Linen thread
- Beeswax
- Needles: embroidery, size 5 and crewel, size 22
- Dark gold passing no. 6, about 6m (6½yd)
- DeVere silk threads (either 6 or 60 – either is fine, as long as you're happy to split the 60s down):
  - Rust
  - Cosmos (60)
  - Crystal white
  - Wine
  - Clementine
  - Ray
  - Gold
  - Liquorice
  - Cornflower
  - Cappuccino
  - Flesh

Working the Background and Border

Unless otherwise stated, use four or five strands of 6, or half a 60, as standard. We're going to use a silk variation of the simple laid and couched work used for both the Bonacon (*see* Chapter 3) and the Hellmouth designs (later in this chapter).

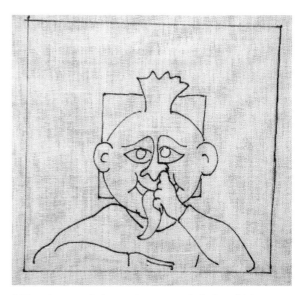

1 Transfer your design to the canvas. As before, it's best to use a permanent marker.

2 Start with eight to ten strands of rust to work the background vertically. This might seem like quite a chunky thread if you're used to the usual two or four strands of opus work, but it's important to get good coverage at this stage – you will still be progressing only one thread of the background canvas as you would with wool, but the canvas is much smaller when working with silks

If you choose to use 60 thread for laidwork, make sure to pull it apart into two bundles of five to loosen the twist. Couch the laidwork with two strands of 6 – if you've used a 60 you will need to pull two strands out to use for this. Remember that because the thread is much finer than that used to work this technique in wool, the couching needs to be closer together at about 3mm (⅛in).

3 Use a whole strand of cosmos in 60 for the bars that create the decorative grid – untwisting it doesn't matter this time because we want it to sit proud of the laidwork rather than blending it, and a bit of twist gives it contrast. We want this to be evenly spaced, so start by putting one bar down the middle at the sides and top. Couch these thick bars using two strands of 6 pulled out from your 60 thread.

4 Place a bar either side of the central one to ensure even spacing. When it comes to the vertical bars across the top and the horizontal bars along the sides, you just have to eyeball the spacing by using the initial long bars as a guide. Make sure the horizontal bars on either side roughly line up with one another (you can use a ruler if you find it helps). Also check that the number of squares you create along the top section is even (there should be an odd number of bars), otherwise the second layer of patterning won't line up.

5 Now take five strands of crystal white, couched with two strands, to make a diagonal grid intersecting with the square grid at the corners. This is spaced so that alternate red squares are plain or have a white cross in the centre. You can nudge the thread into place a little with the couching.

6 Finish the pattern by stitching either a tiny circle or square over the top of each cross. Squares are easier, so it depends how lazy you're feeling. However, if you decide to go for circles I suggest doing a few practice ones before diving into the main piece because unpicking split stitch that's been done on top of laid and couched work is likely to cause wholesale damage to your carefully laid background.

7 Work several densely packed rows of cosmos in four or five strands around the outer edge of the diapered area to form a border. Use the throwing-out technique demonstrated in the Hellmouth project (later in this chapter) to keep the corners sharp. I have worked four rows, but you can make your border thicker or thinner as you please.

The Tunic

Use the layering technique discussed in the Hellmouth project (later in this chapter) to fill out the shapes. Remember to always split something (*see* page 45 for split stitch technique).

8 Outline Sid's tunic in wine. This is mostly one row of stitching, but I've layered in a second row to add shape and depth along his biceps and elbows.

9 Use clementine for the main areas of deep shadow in Sid's tunic. The aim is to leave the areas that will show the shape of the body beneath the clothing, so there are voided ovals to represent his arms and pectoral muscles, plus a small circle for the joint of his elbow.

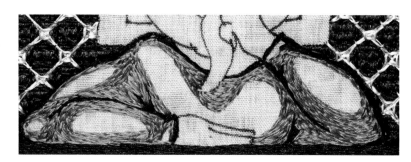

10 Use ray to fill the majority of the muscle shapes, leaving thin areas for the final highlights.

11 Fill in the remaining areas with gold.

Outlining Features and Filling the Eyes

Normally facial symmetry is of vital importance, but with this little charmer it's actually better if his eyes are different sizes and a bit lopsided – it simply adds to his charm.

Our eyes are drawn to the eyes of any human or animal face, so any mistakes here will be especially noticeable. The pupils are such a small area that they are merely the length of a single stitch, so this is one of those rare instances where the use of satin stitch is acceptable in opus anglicanum. Don't worry too much about making the edges neat because we will soon cover them over.

Filling in the Hands and Face

For the rest of the face and hands go down to two strands of 6. Skin is finer and softer then clothing, so it's worked in smaller stitches to show the details properly.

Hands are worked very simply as a series of lines radiating out from the wrist, following the lines of the fingers into their tips.

Faces – even peculiar two colour faces like Sid's – are all about flow and connection, so constantly think about how you can connect one part of the face to another. The lines should always flow into one another.

12 Outline his face and hands with a single row of liquorice.

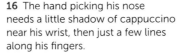

15 The lower hand just needs a few lines of shadow in cappuccino.

16 The hand picking his nose needs a little shadow of cappuccino near his wrist, then just a few lines along his fingers.

13 Use crystal to fill in the whites of his eyes. Make sure to pack the stitches densely and make them flow smoothly around the shape of the eyeballs by using the layering technique.

14 Finish his eyes by working the irises in any colour you choose (I chose cornflower, but they don't have to be blue). Work quite tiny stitches so they flow comfortably around the tight curve, and use the iris colour to cover over any messy edges of the pupil.

17 His fat little neck can be filled in at this stage (I doubt he washes it). Outline two circles for his cheeks, as seen on the right-hand side of his face. Then work a row or two around the outside of the circle, as seen on the left. Work some laughter lines flowing out from under his eyes, and a bit of shading for his chin.

18 Work around the edges of his ears and under his eyebrows. Then split out from the edge of his face, working over the top of his eyebrow.

19 Work right down his nose to outline the bulbous tip, before going over the other eyebrow and splitting into the far side of his face. Work from his ears, over his brows, down into the tip of his nose, back up and over the other brow, and split down into the other ear.

20 Finally, work a couple of rows of stitching around the sides of his baldy bit before connecting the two sides with some lovely, wrinkly laughter lines. I'm not sure if he's laughing with us or at us, but remember to split the lines out from the sides at one side and into them at the other.

21 Still using only two strands, use flesh to fill his hands, working radiating lines out from his wrists into the tips of his fingers.

22 Fill in the rest of his face with the same colour. Remember to think about the flow of the skin, following the lines that are already there and splitting into the cappuccino stitches.

The Mouth, Tongue and Hair

I'm giving Sid a blue tongue like a lizard. You can use pink if you prefer, but the blue will match his eyes and hair to tie the image together.

23 Fill his mouth with wine – the colour, not the liquid. (You can fill your own mouth with the liquid wine, if you like – you deserve a drink for putting up with Sid. Sid prefers lager.)

24 Use two strands of cosmos to outline his tongue at the edges and down the centre.

25 Fill his tongue with the same cornflower blue as his irises.

26 His hair is worked in double stripes of cornflower and ray. I've added an extra part row at the top of each stripe to make his mohawk flare out a little. Make sure to split the hair right out of the flesh of his forehead and down into the border. Work the tips into pointed clumps.

The Square Background

The final step is to fill the central square of background with underside couched gold, using the simplest brick arrangement of the stitch. When you first begin using this stitch, it can be difficult to discern, but as you do more you may find you have a preferred direction in which to work. I will often turn my canvas on its side because I prefer to work away from my body, but I can't do that here because

Sid is sharing his canvas with the Hellmouth and Danse Macabre pieces, so I'm having to work the stitch vertically. If I'm working vertically, I prefer to work from right to left, as I was doing for the first section. No matter how much of this stitch I do, I always feel as though I make a complete bodge of it if I work in the 'wrong' direction. It's worth doing some test patches to figure out your preferred direction of stitching.

27 Work vertically to the image, as is customary with underside couching in period. Whether you start at the top or the bottom, you will quickly come to a point where you will have to work either side of his head. It really doesn't matter which side; just go with the flow.

28 Fill the lower part of the shape. Always work out from the part you've already done, as working two areas of underside couching towards each other can make it very difficult to join them. Begin at the most acute angle – the bit under his ear will only need one strand of gold to fill it, so it's best to start there.

29 Once one gap is filled you can start on the next.

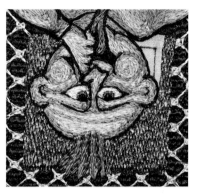

30 At this point I've turned my canvas upside down to finish working the underside couching. (Don't worry about Sid getting dizzy, he says it gives him a new angle to get at the really difficult bogies!) It's always best to start from a straight line if you can, because it's much more difficult to keep the stitches vertical if you're starting from a wonky line, so it makes sense here to invert the canvas so I can start from the other straight edge.

31 Once I've worked as far as I can on one strand of gold, this leaves me with another straight edge to begin the final section...

32 ...which is quite quickly filled.

33 Sid is quite pleased with himself. I hope you are too.

Danse Macabre

The Danse Macabre is based on a series of images by Master Philippe of Geulders, showing death taking many different types of woman. Our skeleton was originally taking the midwife away, but I've changed his dance partner to the elderly debutante because I loved the sense of movement in these two figures. Death looks to me as if he's at his flamenco class, about to shout 'olé'!

Death's original background included a rather flowery wallcovering, which was probably the kind of painted oilcloth seen in wealthy merchant homes, and a chequered tile floor. I kept the floor because my favourite part of or nue embroideries is always the chequered floor, but I've adapted the wallcloth pattern to use another manuscript background, which is easier to sew.

No wallflowers allowed at this dance!

Materials

- Double thickness ramie or linen canvas, about 90 count, at least 30cm (12in) square
- Needles: embroidery size 5, crewel size 22
- Silk 30/2nm thread in yellow
- Collar spacer/button gauge, about 3cm (1¼in) wide, preferably with an angled end (optional but very useful)
- DeVere silk threads, either 6 or 60:
  - Forget me not
  - Wine
  - Crystal white
  - Liquorice
  - Solder
  - Sterling
  - Tinge
  - Constable
  - Cigar
  - Petunia
  - Equator
  - Glace
  - Flesh
- Gold jap thread: k1, approx. 12m (13yd)
- Gold passing thread: no. 6, 1m (39in)

Danse Macabre template. Enlarge by 200%. Finished size 30cm (12in) square.

The Background and Border

Unless otherwise stated, four or five strands of 6 thread are used (half a strand of 60). As before, the background will be laid and couched work (*see* Chapter 3 for detailed laid and couched work instructions). Whether you go vertically or horizontally makes no difference; just be sure to pack the laidwork nice and densely to avoid later gaps.

Spacing and angles are very important with this pattern. I was about to make myself a template strip about 2cm (½in) wide with a 45-degree angle at one end when I realised I had a buttonhole/collar gauge lying around that would do the job perfectly (you can easily make one from a strip of cardboard or thin plastic).

1 Transfer your design to the canvas using a permanent fabric marker.

2 Use eight to ten strands of forget me not blue to fill in the entire upper background. I had a couple of strands go wonky here, but it's fine; once they're couched down they won't be noticeable.

3 Couch this down with two strands of the same colour. Because the silk is very fine, you need the couching bars to be closer together than you would when using a thicker thread-like wool. Here you need to aim for about 3mm (⅛in) spacing.

4 Use a whole strand of wine 60 (keep it twisted in this case) to lay down a diagonal grid with the squares on point to vertical. Using a template at this stage means you can line the grid up perfectly, even when the figures are in the way. It's worth taking time to get this right.

5 Stitch the grid down using two strands for the couching. Once the grid is stable, use your template again to add tiny crossbars in the centre of each square using a whole strand of 60. These don't have to be very long – just one largeish stitch – but they will help you get the next stage looking balanced.

6 The quatrefoils are next, and they aren't as tricky as they look. Start by locating the centre of each square – which should be pretty easy using your crossbars as a guide – and make a small cross using four or five strands of crystal white.

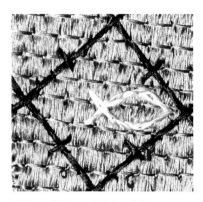

7 Then stitch each lobe of the quatrefoil using the cross as a starting point. They're very small, so it can be helpful to count your split stitches to keep them even: four along each side of the curve is about right for me.

8 Subsequent lobes will only be three on each side because you're building out from the previous stitches, splitting out for each new petal.

9 Work the squares with complete quatrefoils in first, because they're easier and it will help you get the hang of the shape.

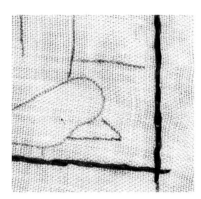

10 Then complete the partial shapes. Don't worry about getting them 100 per cent accurate. As long as the grid is neat, the pattern can cope with a bit of wonky detail.

11 Add a border in four or five strands of the same wine-coloured thread around the edge. Remember with the first few rows to throw the corner stitches out into a cross shape to keep the corners nice and sharp, as in the Bonacon (*see* Chapter 3) and Hellmouth (later in this chapter).

12 Four or five rows around the border ought to be enough, but you can stitch more if you prefer.

The Skeleton

You can shade white with just about any pale colour, but the colour you use will affect the tone of the white. So, if you want your white to look washing powder commercial clean, always shade it with pale blue.

13 Outline the skeleton using liquorice. This is mostly just one row all the way around (the only layering is around his ribs and nasal cavity). Fill his eye as a complete circle. Medieval skeletons are really more cadavers, so we don't need to obsess over the shape of the bones – they're meant to be covered by a layer of shrunken, ghoulish flesh.

14 Outline inside the liquorice lines in grey solder. His arms are quite thin, so the most you can add there is a single row, but his legs are stout enough to accommodate two rows. His torso needs a little layering and sculpting, which mostly follows on from and extends the outline. Ignore his hands and face for now.

15 Again, his arms will only accommodate a single row of pale grey sterling, and his legs a double row. You need to leave a tiny gap for a single row of highlight stitches on his limbs. The pale grey may spread and make it look like you haven't left enough room, but you can always squeeze an extra row in.

His chest needs quite a lot of filling, but remember to leave room for the final colour and always remember to split something. Start each new row by splitting out of a previous one and end each row by splitting into another.

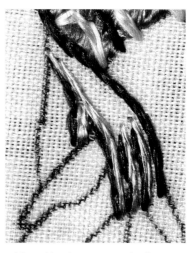

17 Go down to two strands for his hands and face. Hands are pretty simple, especially skeletal ones. Use two strands of sterling to add some shading to the sides of the hands and the fingers – there really isn't much room for any more – following the natural line of the hand bones.

16 Fill in the highlights with tinge.

19 Give the skeleton some teeth before starting on his face. Take ten strands or a full strand of 60 in crystal and sew big stitches along his mouth, intersecting at the jaw. Then couch them down at toothsome intervals using five strands of liquorice, in a decorative version of the couched bars we used earlier for the background. Make sure the liquorice is neat along the edge of the mouth – it's actually better if it overlaps the face a little along the inner edge as it stops the crystal bunching up too much. You can cover the long stitches at the next stage.

18 Fill the hands using two strands of tinge, flowing along the same lines. The fingers will only need one line of each colour.

20 Remember to keep using just two strands for his skull as your stitches will need to be tiny. Use solder to follow the outline of the skull around; it's mostly just one line, but there's a partial second line at the back of his skull and the lower jaw. Fill the nasal cavity and delineate the jaw. Give him two or three dark circles around the eye socket. Remember to always split something (*see* page 45 for split stitch technique).

21 Give the skull a bit of shading in sterling. The lower jaw is almost but not quite filled in – there's still room for a single row of highlight – and I've used some layering to round off the inner part of the shape. His eye socket has a half-moon of shading around the back.

22 Fill in the rest of his skull with two strands of tinge.

23 Go back up to four strands for his shroud, starting with constable. Keep a very light touch here so that his shroud looks whiter than white, because he's out dancing so he's wearing his Sunday best. This is mostly just one row deep, with a couple of partial double rows around the folds near his arm, where the shadows are deepest.

24 Shade the white with the same forget me not blue that we used for the wallpaper. Use a very light touch – never more than two rows deep – because we want white, not blue. Leave plenty of space for the white to dominate.

25 Finally, fill in the rest with crystal white. Following the lines of the folds with just a little bit of layering to accommodate the curves will mean that the stitches reflect the light and give the impression of the folds in the cloth – you're letting light and stitch direction do the modelling for you, rather than trying to use layers of colour. Always remember to split into and out of your previous rows of stitching so that the shroud blends into one piece of cloth.

The Woman

The Gown and Headdress

The wine red overdress (a fitted kirtle is worn beneath) is typical of the late fifteenth century and is known as the gown. You can tell she's French because her hennin headdress is so pointy. (English hennin were shaped more like flowerpots; shorter and blunter than the extremes of continental fashion.)

26 Outline her dress in cigar, adding a little shaping around the folds of drapery, but not too much. This first stage is really about giving a framework to hang the flow of the dress from.

27 The next layer is done in petunia. Again we follow the lines already laid down, extending and thickening them using the layering technique shown later in the Hellmouth project. Where the drapery will be covered by the hem, cuffs or belt of the dress, you can work to a blunt end of each row. Where the ends will be on show, try to split your stitches down to a point (*see* page 45 for split stitch technique), as this will help the visual flow of the cloth.

28 Add a thick layer of equator to join some of the folds together. Again, remember to split into and out of previous rows where necessary, but blunt ends to some of the rows are fine where they will be covered by the cuffs and hem.

29 Fill in the remaining areas with glace.

Making a Dappled Fur Pattern

This type of gown often had a fur lining for warmth (think of the green gown in the Arnolfini Portrait with its sumptuous lining of squirrel). You could fill the cuffs and hem in white and put little black dots on top to represent ermine, but I'm going to use spirals to depict a cheaper fur called astrakhan, or Persian lamb. To do this, we're going to use a variation on the dappling technique.

We need to work a series of tight little spirals, starting with tiny dot of satin stitch, about 3mm (⅛in) square.

Begin to stitch around that square, throwing out the corners to be covered by later rows. Don't try to make the stitches neat. Instead, windmill the stitches out into the surrounding space. This will prevent gaps showing up later.

Continue working around in an outward spiral, throwing the stitches out. Let them overlap a little and let the texture build up.

As the spiral gets bigger, your stitches will naturally round themselves out.

30 Fill the hem and cuffs with circles, working each one out until it touches its neighbour.

31 Give each area of fur a definite edge with a single row of stitching.

32 Fill in the background by first working out from the spirals towards any untouched edges, always splitting into and out of the existing stitches, then finally filling in with a small triangular split stitch.

33 Use a few stitches of constable to fill the spots where the lining of the cuffs shows.

34 Outline and shade her collar and the hood around her face with liquorice.

35 Then fill the remainder with constable.

36 Use ten strands of constable to put down small areas of laidwork for her wide belt and the point of her hennin headdress.

37 Use a single strand of gold passing to lay down a trellis (just like the trellis couching used in Chapter 3 for the Bonacon) over the silk. Be gentle; not only can the passing catch very easily, but so can the silk. Passing is bouncier and much less bendy than silk thread, so don't worry too much if it won't go exactly where you want it to – as long as it's in roughly the right place, you'll be able to gently nudge it back into place at the next stage.

38 Use four strands of either glace or equator (petunia is a bit too dark to contrast well) to couch the points of the gold trellis. I used a single stitch on her hennin and a cross or two stitches on her belt. Remember, this is when you can nudge any unruly gold thread back into line.

The Hands and Face

Use just two strands for the flesh of her face and hands. Her hands are really just an impressionistic series of straight lines. They are too small to hold much detail, so don't worry if she only has three fingers because you didn't have room for four. It's fine, no one will ever notice, apart from that one annoying uncle who has to pick fault with everything, and you have to give him something to keep him happy.

I used to leave the mouths of opus faces as severe little black lines, but then it occurred to me that paler pinks fade faster and that some faces do have some shaped stitches around that severe little line. So I began to experiment with adding a hint of lip colour to restore what might have been lost. I am always wary of introducing new colours that will only be used once, because medieval embroidery is very economical in its use of colour, so here I used the dark red petunia leftover from her dress. I was worried it might be a bit much, but I think I love it – it gives her a gothic hint of Morticia Addams.

A high forehead was a desirable attribute for a young woman wearing this type of headdress, to the point that many courtly ladies plucked their foreheads. No trace of hair would be visible.

39 Outline her hands in the same liquorice as her dress. Then fill them from the wrist down to the fingertips in a series of straight lines, in much the same way as her dance partner's hands.

40 Finish outlining her face in liquorice. It's best to use five strands for this stage because the dark lines will often be compressed by the stitching of the skin. It's just one row throughout, apart from her eyebrows, which are done with two.

41 Fill in the whites of her eyes using a spot of crystal white.

42 She needs little more than a single stitch of forget me not to add colour to her eyes. Add a touch of petunia to colour her lips. This doesn't need to be more than four stitches on a face this size – two top and two bottom.

43 Go down to two threads for her flesh, starting with her décolletage. Medieval artists would have been appalled by the modern obsession with big boobs, so there's no discernible cleavage going on here. Outline her clavicle and the tendons of her neck in three graceful interlocking arcs.

44 Fill these by following the flow of the skin, and then outline her cheeks, making sure that they are level.

The Symmetry of the Face

Symmetry is an essential component of human beauty, and she is meant to be fair and damned, so it's worth double checking this.

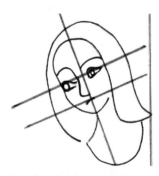

Level does not mean level along a true horizontal or vertical line to the image. If I impose true vertical and horizontal over the image, you can see that the image is askew.

Every face has its own horizontal and vertical, which can be at odds with those of the overall image. The vertical line of a face runs down the central line of the forehead, nose and lips. The horizontal lines are set by the eyes and mouth. 'Level' for our face means that the eyes should be in line and evenly sized; the cheeks should line up with the lips at the bottom, touch the lower eyelid at the top, and fill the area between nose and the side of face.

45 Fill her cheeks by spiralling round towards the centre (you will eventually come to a point where all you need are a couple of stitches in the middle), then split out of the side of the cheek spiral to work up under the brow, outlining the nose.

46 Fill underneath each brow – the far brow is filled in much the same way – and then split out from the brow and work across the top of her high, domed forehead.

47 Use layering to fill her forehead down towards her brows. Split out from the lower cheek and work along the outline of her jaw before circling around under her nose and back into her cheek.

48 The last task is to fill all of the little gaps left behind when the dominant shapes have been filled. Take care to split out of and then into the stitches that are already there so that the silk blends together into one cohesive piece of skin.

There is never any shame in realizing you've left a tiny gap and going back to fix it with an extra stitch or two, as I've just done when I noticed a gap in her neck as I enlarged the photo.

The Dancefloor

Embellishing with Gold

For the or nue floor that the dancers prance upon, I'm going to use jap gold rather than passing. Although I've used the term or nue to describe the couched gold floor, it's a very simple form, and could really just be called decorative surface couching, since all we're doing is holding the gold down with two different colours.

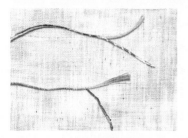

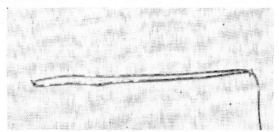

The jap thread is the one at the top of the picture, and passing is below. As you can see, the jap is a broader wind around the core thread, and it's gilded paper rather than a metallic plastic. This means it's a bit trickier to get the thread through fabric as it sheds more easily, but because it's softer it's much easier to bend it around a corner, so it's much easier for medieval or nue.

All we're basically going to do here is couch down gold thread in a decorative manner, but just as with the underside couching, the gold will be used as continuous thread. (You can usually see the neat returns at the edges of medieval or nue pieces.) The gold will be couched in pairs of threads, so the first thing to do is to lay down a bar of double gold threads. Stretch out a gold thread across the area to be filled, then surface couch down the return point at the other end – whether or not you couch both ends is up to you; I prefer to do so because it helps the gold behave. Don't worry if it looks a bit askew at this stage, you will be able to nudge it down when you couch.

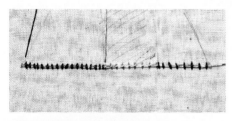

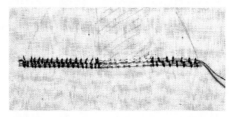

Use four or five strands of two different colours – I've used constable and tinge for a not quite black-and-white effect – and couch down the gold in a checked pattern. How closely you space your coloured couching stitches will influence the finished pattern. Here I've done my couching very close together on the left and wider on the right.

Lay one row of gold, couch it down and then lay the next layer of gold on top, using the couching stitches to pull the rows of gold close and tight together.

49 You may find it helpful to sketch in alternate tiles to help you keep track of the colours.

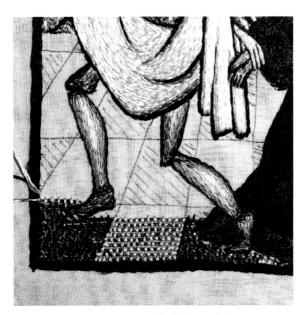

50 I always find it helpful to work the least noticeable areas first in order to get any mistakes out of the way, so I'm going up the right-hand side of the image first.

51 As with the underside used for Hellmouth (*see* next project) and Sid (earlier in this chapter), this type of couching isn't going to bend around any corners, so when you come to an obstacle you have to choose a side and work up that way before coming back to complete the other side. Which side you do first is normally dictated by random chance because it's whichever side your thread happens to be on. I'm sure there must be some people who can work these things out in advance, but I'm not that clever.

52 And they're ready to dance the night away!

Hellmouth

This design is based on a twelfth-century enamelled altarpiece attributed to the Belgian artist, Nicholas of Verdun. Hell was a common theme in medieval art, and to be honest I like both the profusion of bare bottoms in this version and the demons. (I do like embroidering medieval demons!) It also appealed to me as a silversmith because I've worked several pieces in this champlevé style of enamel and know how difficult they are.

I've simplified the design somewhat by omitting a few damned faces to make the design work with a reasonably sized canvas. I've also used some modern coloured passing threads to echo the lovely bright red enamels of the original. My choice of red for the centre of the flames, edged with gold, is directly copied from the glorious red enamel of the original, but it did lead to a somewhat heated physics debate with my photographer, who insisted it should be the other way around 'because that's how flames work'.

Buffy couldn't make it, and Sam and Dean were busy!

Although this design is worked in an opus anglicanum style, it uses the same laid and couched work as the earlier Bonacon design (*see* Chapter 3) used in wool, in the style of later pieces of opus anglicanum. It's much trickier to work this stitch in silk than in wool, but as with wool you need to use a thicker thread for the initial laid part of the stitch, which is why I've recommended the Devere 60 thread.

As I was working I noticed that only one of the damned is discernibly female in appearance, and this is about the same gender ratio as in the original. This not particularly unusual in medieval art, which has a tendency to favour the male image, but it did strike me as odd given the propensity of medieval religion to lay all sin at the door of womankind. Curious, I did an internet search to find out what proportion of the prison population of the Western world is female, to see if this medieval depiction of sinners reflected rates of female crime in our own time, and came up with a worldwide figure of just under 7 per cent, with variations of a rate of 4 per cent in the UK and 8 per cent in the US. So, if anything, one female face out of seven gives a rate of roughly 14 per cent, or twice the rate of modern female crime, and a distinct overrepresentation of women for once! Obviously, the ladies were all too busy doing their embroidery to cause trouble.

You can, of course, work this design in other types of silk, but if you don't use a filament (also known as reeled or flat silk), then the results won't be opus anglicanum. Only filament silk brings light into the stitching; twisted silk won't bring light in the same way and cotton brings none at all. To understand opus anglicanum, you need to understand the role of light and the way it reflects upon the silk to shape flat stitches into the appearance of three dimensions.

Materials

- Double-layered ramie or linen canvas, roughly 90 count, minimum size: 40cm (16in) square
- Needles: embroidery, size 5; chenille, size 22
- Linen thread
- Beeswax
- DeVere silks (either 6 or 60, unless otherwise stated use four or five strands of 6/half a strand of 60):
  - Neptune (60)
  - Gold (60)
  - Rust (60)
  - Dark slate
  - Cigar
  - Crystal white
  - Myrtle
  - Cactus
  - Linden
  - Sea blue
  - Tinge
  - Glace
  - Carrot
  - Buddleia
  - Hyacinth
  - Lilac
  - Flesh
- Passing thread (6):
  - Dark gold, 10m (11yd)
  - Copper, 7m (75/8yd)
  - Black, 1m (39in)
  - Dark red, 22m (24yd) (bright red is fine, if you prefer)

Hellmouth template. Enlarge by 200%. Finished size 40cm (16in) square.

The Background and Border

We start with the gorgeous blue background in laid and couched work. This is the same technique as used in Chapter 3 for the Bonacon design, but here it's used in silk, as was often the case in later-style opus anglicanum. The theory is that it's quicker to fill a large blank space with this stitch than with packed split stitch, but in practice laid and couched work with flighty filament silks isn't as much of a time saver as you think it's going to be, although it does make a nice textural contrast with the rest of the work.

Split Stitch in Opus Anglicanum

The split stitch used in opus anglicanum is exactly the same as the split stitch used with wool in Chapter 2 (*see* page 45 for split stitch technique). However, filament silk has its own little quirks, which I will try to highlight as we go along. Rather than using split stitch as an outlining stitch, we are going to use it here as a filling stitch, so packing the stitches becomes very important, as does the flow of stitching.

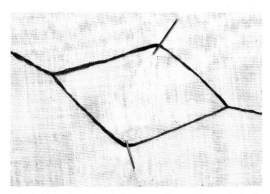

DeVere 60 (top) and 6 (below).

This thread is basically ten strands of the 6 weight, loosely twisted, which can be split down into two bunches of five strands. When working drapery it can be lot easier to split a 60 strand in half than to strand out four or five individual strands of 6. For the laid and couched background, ten strands is about right, but it's best to use half a 60 doubled over because pulling five strands out from the bundle loosens the twist, and twist is the enemy of shine.

If – as with the blue neptune thread for the laid and couched work background – you want a single or pair of 6 threads in the same colour, there is no need to buy a second reel of thread in a different weight, because you can just pull a single out from the bundle of ten, just as you would with stranded cotton floss.

As before, we need to use a thicker thread to cover the background, so use a 60 thread in neptune. Reel out a very long strand, because you will be doing ridiculously long stitches, then pull five strands out from the bundle of ten to loosen the twist and double them over in your needle.

1 Transfer the design to your canvas. Use a permanent fabric marker – preferably fine line. Don't be tempted to use a fade-out or wash-out pen – you won't finish this design before the ink fades, and washing the finished piece is ill-advised. Pencil is also a bad idea as the graphite can rub off and muddy the silk colours.

2 Work long stitches of neptune all the way from the top to bottom of the piece. Remember to pack them together to compensate for the spreading stitches (in the same way as in the earlier woolly projects). You can also join the laid threads as I demonstrated for the laidwork border of the Bonacon piece in Chapter 3, which I also demonstrate in Chapter 6 of my *Bayeux Stitch* book.

3 Pull two strands to use for the couching. Because this thread is finer than that used for the wool version of this stitch, the couching bars also need to be closer together; about 3mm (⅛in) is right.

Remember to check the spread of the laidwork at the sides and pull it back into line with your couching. The longer the span of a single stitch, the more likely it is to wander away from the line, but you can nudge it back with your couching thread.

4 Use four or five strands of gold to work around the edge of the blue laid and couched work. How many circuits you do is up to you; I went for three gold in total, but you can do more if you prefer a thicker border.

When you come to the sharp right-angled corners, throw your stitches out a little and overlap them, rather than trying to work neatly around the corner. Throwing the corners out a little keeps them nice and sharp with each layer, defying their tendency to round off. Only your final two rows need neat corners to cover the previous rows. (This is also demonstrated in the Bonacon project in Chapter 3.)

5 Work four or five strands of rust around the edges of the gold. Again, I've done four rows of stitching around, but this is a matter of personal preference.

Just as you can throw the right-angled corners out to ensure coverage and a sharp angle, you may want to stitch right into the upper angles where the curves meet – it's better to overlap your stitches than to have gaps appear later. (There is never any shame in realising you've left a gap and going back to fill it. Just remember to split your repair into and out of the existing stitches so they blend.)

6 Finally, go around again with the gold, remembering this time to neaten up the corners. I went around twice, but you can do more if you wish.

Layering

When you want to thicken out a line or a shape, work the first part of the line, shown here in red, along the part you want thickening (about two-thirds of the way along in this case). Then carry your needle over the back of the work and split a new stitch out of the row. Work along the top and slope back down where the first row of stitching ends.

So, the ends of the row of stitching are a single row deep and the middle is two rows deep. By layering this technique into multiple rows, you can radically alter the

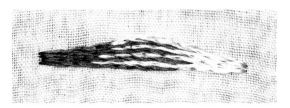

I've worked this sample in two colours to show the principle, but in practice you will use a single colour.

shape of a line or curve, while maintaining the smooth flow of light over your stitches. Split out of the previous row of stitches and back into it again at the end of each row. You should never see a blunt end to a row of stitches in opus anglicanum as this interrupts the visual flow.

The Beast

It's time to start on the big beastie with all of hell in his mouth. He has a lovely big mouth – all the better to eat you with! Reusing the same colours several times in the same piece is one of the ways to make it look more medieval and harmonious. If you throw all the colours in your threadbox at it, it will look a mess.

Always remember to split something: split your new row out of an old one when you begin, and split down into a previous row to end it. You should never see a single stitch in opus anglicanum.

7 Use four or five strands of dark slate to outline the beast's brow, eye and nose. For the brow I've used two rows, fading into one at the narrow part of his jaw. For the jaw I used just one line, thickened to two at the central part, using the layering technique shown above.

His nostril is also worked in three rows of layered stitches, as is his outer snout. The curl of his nose is also layered out.

8 Use four or five strands of cigar to work a spiral for his eyeball. You will get more accurate placement of the spiral if you work from the outside towards the centre, as this allows you to establish a firm edge.

9 Use the same rust as the border – again in four or five strands – to add the pupil, which I worked with two rows of stitch. Then add a nice red rim around the outside of his eye (because 99 per cent of demons have a permanent hangover) and a little highlight of rust around the spiral of his nose.

10 Use crystal white for the whites of his eyes, taking care to really pack your stitches together and make them flow smoothly around the shape of the eyeball. Our eye is naturally drawn to the eyes of any image, so any discrepancies or messy stitches will show more around the eyes than in any other part of your stitching.

11 I've chosen myrtle for the next layer of skin because it has such a lovely oily quality that's perfect for demons. You don't need to follow the previous line exactly, and here I've chosen to mostly ignore the line around his mouth, just adding a small amount of myrtle to emphasise the spiral of his nose. I've added the largest part of this colour to the midsection of his face (the part with the eye), with one layer around the top and several rows around his eye, layered a little to smooth out the curve. In the bottom layer, I added one of two rows towards the tip of the jaw, but several more to emphasise his brow.

12 Cactus forms the next layer of colour, worked much more heavily so that it dominates.

I still haven't touched the line nearest his mouth, but I've worked an extra layer on top of the myrtle ones, again using the layering technique shown above to allow the shape of his face to flow and curve in an organic fashion. I've also added an extra wrinkle to his snout.

13 The final shade of green is linden, which is basically used to fill in the rest of his face, working with the flow of the previous stitches.

14 Work a couple of rows of sea blue for the lip.

15 Then add a single row of tinge for the edge of the lip.

16 His beard is worked in sea blue and rust, in alternating stripes. Either two or three rows in each colour is fine. (You could even go for four, if you prefer, but don't be tempted to work single rows as they won't stand out enough and the colour will get muddy. You need a certain boldness for opus hair – it's very cartoonish.)

Split each row out of the edge of his face to avoid any gaps – the beard needs to look like it's growing out of his face. Split the end of each group of coloured stitches into a point so they look like the growing end of a hair – demons get very self-conscious about their split ends.

17 Have some fun and play with the hair in his beard to add some waves, and then work his little spiky mohawk in the same way.

The Flames

Outline the flames next. Don't feel that you have to follow my arrangement of colours, which was dictated by when my thread ran out as I wanted a certain random element here. Make your own random arrangement.

18 Add just a single row of outline stitching. I've used a mixture of rust, gold, glace and carrot, but you can go for a single colour if you prefer. These outline stitches will only show a tiny bit in the finished piece, and the aim of working them in four different colours is to add a little flickering quality to the sparkling metal threads.

The Demon

A confession – Maurice here (his name is Maurice, by the way) was going to be a rather conservative golden brown, but as soon as I put the first stitch of brown in place he expressed his desire to be a fabulous giant purple people eater, and I'm too scared of him to argue, so he's purple. And fabulous, obviously.

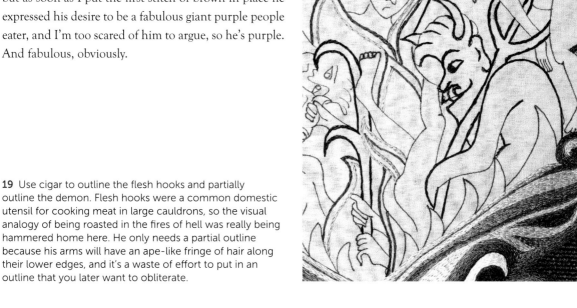

19 Use cigar to outline the flesh hooks and partially outline the demon. Flesh hooks were a common domestic utensil for cooking meat in large cauldrons, so the visual analogy of being roasted in the fires of hell was really being hammered home here. He only needs a partial outline because his arms will have an ape-like fringe of hair along their lower edges, and it's a waste of effort to put in an outline that you later want to obliterate.

20 Add a triangle of crystal white to his eye.

21 Then some touches of rust for his iris, eyeliner, upper brow, ear and lips.

22 Use buddleia to add the first layer of shadow to his body and arm. Mostly this is a case of defining the highlighted shapes of his muscles and belly, then filling in the rest using flowing lines of stitch, remembering to split in and out. His paw needs a quite a light touch at this stage.

23 Use hyacinth for the middle layer of shading. I've completely filled the upper arm behind his head because it's in shadow, but for the rest I've used two or three rows of stitch, often a little asymmetrically to show the light radiating from the flames in the centre of the images.

24 Fill the rest in with lilac, remembering to follow the flow of the shapes and always split something.

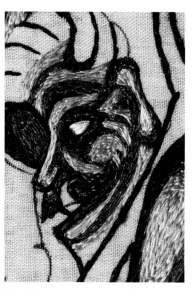

25 Go down to two strands for his face. Start with buddleia, using quite a light touch. Add some half-moons of shadow around the base of his horn. Re-emphasise his eyeliner and work it outwards from the corner into a few crow's feet. Outline his lip and give a touch of shadow inside his ear.

26 The second layer is hyacinth. Be bold here, his face is meant to be grotesque and scary, and lines are quite reminiscent of those on a Japanese Kabuki mask – think drama! Anyone this purple is bound to be a bit of a drama queen, after all.

The lines you leave for the pale colour need to be clear and flowing, so draw more lines out from his crow's feet, give him a prominent naso-labial line, let a clear line flow around his underbrow and right down his nose, give him a good fat lip and a little apple for his cheek.

27 Fill in the stripes with lilac, following the flow established by the first layer. His look is almost complete.

28 Stitch his hair in alternating double rows of cactus and tinge. Remember to split the hair out of his flesh, just the way hair grows. Split the tips together into clumps, and have some fun with it. If you want to add piercings, do this at the very end with a spot of surface couched gold or silver.

The Bodies

Dubious, shady types like Maurice are represented in medieval art by two tone skins, but the flesh of ordinary folk, like the ones falling into the Hellmouth, is depicted all in one colour. The stitches are done in such a way as to shape the flesh, and there is quite a lot of flesh on show here.

Always remember that when starting a new row of stitching, you should split it out of a previous row or shape, and when ending the row you split it back into a previous row. This will blend the shapes together and make them look like a single piece of skin rather than a random assemblage of flesh-coloured shapes.

29 Now for the bare arses! Start by outlining them in dark slate.

30 Work in four or five strands of flesh for the bodies. We're going to start by modelling the large muscle groups (mostly buttocks and thighs in this case). I find it helps to think of the bodies as robot parts with circular joints at elbows and knees as components making up a human-type body.

Define the outer part of each shape, be that a perfectly circular arse cheek or elongated shin or thigh. Really push the edge right up against the outline to make the flesh look full and round. Then work in a spiral toward the centre until the shape is filled completely – you will come to a point where the central gap is best filled by just a couple of split stitches because there isn't room to spiral round any further.

On the skinnier bodies to the left, you have separate buttocks and thighs, but on the plumper carcass Maurice is spearing, thigh and bum have become a single round shape due to the slumped posture. There are also elbows, knees, a foot, a belly, shins and upper arms to be filled with smooth, rounded shapes.

31 Once you've got the hang of filling the complete, smoothly-shaped muscle groups, it's time to move on to the partial ones – a shoulder in the upper left, a few partial buttocks, a partial thigh, some ribcages and even a partial shin.

Where the shapes are close together, try and let them touch if you can do so, while letting the shapes make sense. (So the sticking-up bottom in the lower left quadrant has the thigh muscle worked right up against it, but the chest cavity right next to it doesn't quite touch because your ribs don't go all the way down to your arse.)

You can work some shapes, like the partial buttocks, as distorted spheres, but others like the shin that's tucked under Maurice's beard are better worked as though they are partly covered (which, in this case, it is).

32 Work on filling in the rest of the flesh by joining the larger shapes together using flowing lines of stitch.

The top-left chap, who is just a head and shoulders, needs to have his neck extended out by splitting out of the shoulder mound and working along his spine, before finishing his skin below the flesh hook.

The bum people will also benefit from having their spines defined by a few straight rows of stitching that split out of their buttocks and back into their rib cages, before carefully filling the triangular gaps by following the flow of the shapes.

Flailing legs person is very similar, but with the addition of some long straight rows between shin and ankle.

Pitchfork has some fiddly bits to fill in around the ankles and knees, but his back is the main area to be filled. As before, work a good few straight lines along his back to suggest his spine, but then start working around the lumpy bits of belly and chest until you make a triangular gap where belly and spine meet. After you've filled that gap, you will have an impression of creased skin where he bends in the middle. His forearm isn't really worth shaping, so that's best filled with straight lines.

33 Sometimes it's hard to see the point of all this careful shaping when the picture is taken flat, but as you can see from this photo taken at an angle, the light reflecting on the silk shapes creates some quite dramatic and effective modelling. An image done in opus will move with the light.

The Hands and Faces

All hands are single outline in four strands. All faces are single outline in four strands, but with a double row for the eyebrows. Eyeballs can be done in satin stitch. Note that you don't need to outline any part of the face or hands that will be covered, either by hair or by a neighbouring shape. Don't worry, medieval artists couldn't draw hands either.

As I noted in the Danse Macabre project, facial symmetry is a defining aspect of beauty. However, that is not really a major concern with the faces in this image as they're meant to be the poor tortured damned having nasty things done to their nether regions in Hades because they've been very naughty boys and girls – especially the members of the clergy present, because they're supposed to know better.

When I teach people how to do opus anglicanum faces, I always say that every face is different, but the same rules apply to all, and this is a perfect example of that. I've made several of my faces a bit cross-eyed, as I imagine terrible things are happing to their nether regions out of shot. You can just leave the mouths as a dark line, which I often used to do as this is how they look in the originals. However paler colours of the kinds used for lips tend to fade very quickly, so you can add some speculative lip colour if you prefer.

34 Begin by outlining the hands and faces. You can use either dark slate or cigar. I used a bit of both because my dark slate ran out halfway through and I was too lazy to get up and find another reel.

35 Hands are really easy to fill, so it's best to start with them (that way you get used to using two strands instead of one before moving on to the faces, where mistakes are far more noticeable). At their simplest, like the hands to the left, all that's needed is to fill with a series of straight lines, moving from wrist to fingertips.

Curled hands are filled in much the same way, but sometimes with separate fingertips, as with those in the centre.

The final hand at the top is shown palm outwards. In this case, you might want to try defining the pad of the thumb and palm by using stitch direction.

36 Start by filling the whites of the eyes using crystal. Work a triangular group of stitches along the outline of the eye with filling stitches between. You can use four strands for the whites. Shine is the important part here, as it helps to shape the eyeball.

37 Add some colour to the eyes. This is usually just a single stitch using four strands, which covers the iris. You can use any colour you like – I used the dark blue neptune from the background and cactus green.

Add some lip colour. This doesn't need to be more than two or three stitches on either side of the mouth, split into the dark line at the ends to give shape. I've mostly used the rust colour from the border, but for the lady and the poor fella kissing arse I've used bright glace red and made their lips extra pouty, because they need to pucker up!

38 The cheeks are the defining shape of any face, so begin by outlining these. The profile faces only need one cheek, so balance isn't an issue, but as a general rule it's a good idea to split out of the neck to begin the cheek, so as to blend the areas into something that looks like skin. Fill as much of the cheek space as you can, working right alongside the lines of the side of the face, lower eye and nose, while keeping the shape nice and round.

For the monk, you can bring a line up along the sinew of his neck to begin the spiral, but the bishop's neck isn't visible. Both need a partial spiral for their turned-away cheeks.

The guy with the hook in his face looks better with imbalanced cheeks, but the lady will look better if you make her face symmetrical.

Purse guy, at the top of the pile, can have his neck coloured in at any point, which I've done here.

39 Continue the cheek spirals inward until they're full. Then split out of the side of the cheek where possible to work a line below the brow and down the nose.

This is relatively straightforward in the three-quarter profile faces, but in the full-profile faces you may have to fudge it a bit, working a bit of brow and a separate nose.

At this point, I realised I'd made a minor mistake in my original drawing and added a tiny bit of blue laid and couched work to the side of the neck of the man at the top. This has been corrected for you in the version shown here.

Working an Inward Spiral

When working an inward spiral, like the cheeks, it helps to just nibble the outer spiral with each descending line, as shown here in my expanded stitch diagram. Nicking into the outer line stops the spiral pulling in towards the centre too much, which can create gaps.

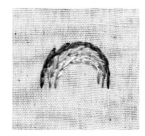
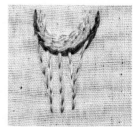

When your spiral becomes a cheek and you need to blend it with the jawline, it helps to think of the jawline stitches as supporting the ball of the cheek like fingertips holding a ball. Use layering to splay the stitches out into a supporting shape, and then split the ends into the ball.

40 Fill both under brow areas on each face before beginning the forehead, working up from the brows into the hairline. Often, I will work straight across the brows without dipping between them at all, to give the serene untroubled look that is the hallmark of so many medieval saints. But, let's face it, if any of this lot were even remotely saintly, they wouldn't be in this pickle in the first place. They are all deeply troubled indeed, so I've allowed my stitches to dip quite savagely between their brows to make them frown.

I also filled in the monk's neck and outlined the musculature of the lady's décolletage.

41 Continue to work the forehead until it just about meets the hairline. Don't worry too much about any drawings of the hair at this point, you can work over them and reinstate them later – they're only there as a guideline.

Work the monk's tonsure. You can outline his baldy bit if you want to, but I tend not to bother.

On each figure, work a line that outlines the shape of the lower face. This one is variable, since with the profile faces all you really want is a line along the jaw and another that goes under the cheek and nose. However, with the three-quarter faces this becomes more of a circle that defines the chin and naso-labial lines (sort of a muzzle).

Fill the lady's décolletage by following the lines laid down previously.

42 Fill in all of the remaining gaps, taking care to blend the stitches along the direction of the previous rows. Always split your new stitches out of and then back into the previous rows to blend the skin into one flesh.

Working Two-Coloured Stripes

This opus anglicanum is made from stripes of two colours. You use any two colours you like, just so long as they have a reasonable amount of contrast. Opus anglicanum was never meant to be examined in the microscopic detail with which we examine the original pieces today.

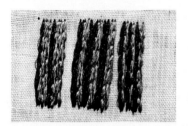

By far the most common arrangement for opus anglicanum stripes is two rows of one and two of the other (middle). One row plus two (right) also works, but one and one (left) becomes blurry and indistinct – remember, you need to be able to make out the hair from at least 2m (6ft) away.

The Hair

You can use any colours you like for the hair, as long as they contrast well, but I would always advise against introducing a whole new colour unless it's strictly necessary. I've used combinations of the colours I've already used to create harmony, as follows:

43 Gold and tinge. Tinge is one of those wonderfully malleable colours that changes completely depending on what you combine it with.

44 Dark slate and rust.

45 Dark slate and tinge.

46 Dark slate and cigar.

47 Rust and cigar.

48 Gold and carrot. This combination is a bit close in tone, but I wanted her to be a luxuriant brassy blonde because I think she's meant to have been damned for her vanity. I'm not sure if her hair is flipping up like that because the flames have caught it or just because she's worth it.

49 Gold and rust.

The Purse

I think the purse is there to suggest that he is damned for usury, the practice of lending money for interest. This was forbidden to Christians in the medieval era, resulting in the difficult relationship between European royalty and the Jews, who were left with moneylending as just about the only way they could earn a living.

50 Outline his purse in four strands of myrtle, with a little bit of shading to round out the base. Make sure the base of the purse touches the head of the woman below so you don't leave yourself with an awkward, hard to fill gap.

51 Round out the shading with some cactus.

52 Fill the remainder with linden.

The Bishop's Mitre

You get a lot of clergymen in medieval hell – perhaps it's because they used the benefit of their positions and the favour of the church courts to get away with most crimes in real life. For a long time, man could claim 'benefit of clergy' in an English court just by proving he could read Latin, and thus be tried instead in the far more lenient church court.

53 Outline the bishop's mitre with four strands of buddleia.

54 Fill the bands on the upper part of the mitre with split stitched hyacinth, but fill the band in laidwork.

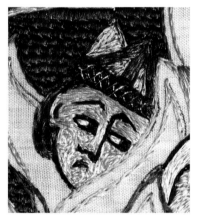

55 Use a short length of dark gold passing thread to carefully work a trellis over the laid band of his mitre, couching the points with hyacinth silk, then fill the central triangles and the back of the mitre with lilac.

The Beast's Teeth

You can use cigar or dark slate to outline the teeth if you prefer, but I'm going with gold for a subtle hint of nicotine staining – you can tell he's a smoker. For filling the teeth, I used crystal white – a bluey bright white – as I want his teeth and eyes to glow in the gloom at the bottom of the image, but you can use a softer white if you prefer.

56 Outline the beastie's teeth in gold.

57 Fill his teeth with four strands of crystal white.

The Pitchforks and Flesh Hooks

When used as a background filling, underside couching is pretty much always worked vertically to the main image, but with smaller areas like these it's fine to work along the straight line of the object in question. I rotated my frame between working the pitchfork and the hook so I could work each in my easiest direction. It's often better to concentrate on the small area you need to fill rather than obsessing over having the image the correct way up.

58 Use copper passing, underside couched, for the pitchfork and flesh hook.

For the flesh hook, you can work along the main shaft as one piece, but you will have to start a new strand for the lower hook. The upper hook is separated from the main shaft and is just about thin enough to be worked with curved underside couching, as long as you take care to keep the stitches small so they don't overlap.

I worked the main shaft of the pitchfork from right to left, because that's my preferred and most comfortable direction for this stitch. This has left a straight line worked along the central tine and out into the left-hand tine. The tines in this case aren't worked in curved couching because they are joined onto the straight bits, and underside couching just doesn't work that way.

59 In both cases, when you come to fill out the various hooks and tines, work out from the previous rows of stitch. It's really hard to get a good join by working two areas of underside couching so they meet in the middle, so why make life more difficult for yourself?

60 I started with the copper because the shapes are relatively simple. You should stop and appreciate how pretty the copper is for a minute. I think I like it more than gold.

The Demon's Horns, Tusk and Claws

Maurice's horns, tusk and claws are next. Now you've got into the swing of things with the underside couching, you should be able to cope with how fiddly these are to do. I've used black passing but, of course, you could use any colour that takes your fancy. Maurice is very vain about his horns and has a collection of nail polishes so he can change the colours on a regular basis and he won't mind at all.

Working Narrow Areas of Underside Couching

It can be tempting when working very narrow areas of underside couching to simply go back and forth in a kind of metallic version of satin stitch, as in the left-hand sample. However this will make the narrow areas stand out because their texture will be different – and much shinier – than the rest of the underside couching. It's also much more likely that these stitches will twist.

The middle bar shows a narrow area worked with one stitch straight across, alternating with one couched in the middle to maintain the same texture as the body of the couching.

The right bar shows a couching stitch a third of the way along each row, alternating between left and right, which maintains the texture even better than the middle.

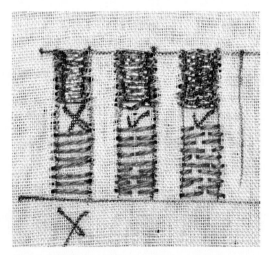

In reality, if you're working a descending shape like the pointed hook, you're probably going to use a combination of both the centre and right techniques as you work into the point.

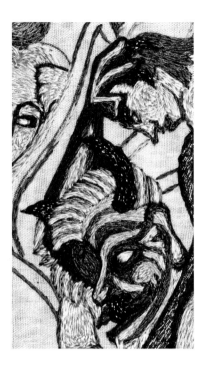

61 All can be worked on a slight curve, as long as you keep the stitches a bit smaller than usual, although his horns are on the upper limit of the width of space that can be comfortably worked as a curve.

Outlining and Filling the Flames

The next step is to fill the narrow channels around the edge of each flame in dark gold underside couching. You will need to concentrate on keeping the stitches on the short side most of the time so they curve neatly. If you choose dark red for the filling, it needs to be treated with a little extra care because it is more loosely wound than some of the other passings. The black core of the thread shows through to add that lovely dark edge, but it also means it tends to fray more easily.

Once you've done a bit of underside couching, you will probably find you have a preferred direction of stitch. If I'm working vertically, I find right to left much easier and as I far prefer to work horizontally away from my body, when working a large piece like this I will often place it on its side to make stitching easier. However, it's not always possible to do that with a piece like this (unless you want to spend your time twirling your frame around like a majorette's baton) so there will be times when you'll have to work against your preference and will have to pay more attention to what you're doing.

62 Start along the inside of each shape because when you come to the point of each curve you will be able to fill them better if you work out. Where you reverse direction at the points, the gold thread is going to try and pull into the curve. Working out from the centre of the point allows you to easily layer up the stitches and ensure good coverage, whereas if you try and work from the outer point, you will be trying to force your stitches under the previous row and it will be harder to get decent coverage.

63 Some of the shorter bits are pretty straightforward, but there are lots of curvy wiggly bits to keep you on your toes.

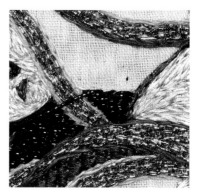

64 Once the gold is done, the final step is to fill the flames with red. Underside couching for large areas of fill is almost always worked on a strict vertical to the main image. Sometimes this is pretty easy because you have a straight edge to start from, but that isn't always the case with these wobbly shapes, so you have to make a decision with each flame. Sometimes, as here, there will be a short but reasonably vertical edge to start from, or if you're confident you can often impose a short straight stitch upon the side to a large curve.

66 We're all finished!

65 Not everyone is brilliant at judging angles. If the thought of finding a straight part of a curve fills you with dread, the alternative is to begin in the middle, seen here from left to right.

Start by drawing a vertical line at the tallest part of your shape (taking the longest line possible is always easier than worrying about where dead centre is). Work out from that line until the first section is full. Then go back to the line and work out from it in the other direction.

Do not try to work your second section from the outline towards the central line; work out from the existing stitches instead. It's tricky to get the stitches to meet neatly in the middle, and there is no point making life harder than it needs to be.

CHAPTER 7

WHITEWORK

Whitework was used for a lot of altar cloths and chalice veils as well as a few surviving antependia in the Middle Ages. Most of the surviving pieces are of Germanic origin, making this a technique that is primarily classed as opus teutonicum rather than opus anglicanum. Worked in linen on linen, the appeal of whitework would have been its washability, in contrast to the delicate wools and silks of laid and couched work or opus anglicanum, making it ideal for items that were likely to have communion wine or molten beeswax spilled upon them.

I love the idea of rude images contrasting with the virgin purity of white, which is why I've worked the pieces here. Some of the techniques are employed elsewhere in this book, which is why I've put these chapters at the end. However, there are a few other stitches to be introduced at this point, which – although they may be quite familiar to the experienced modern stitcher – seem only to be used for whitework in this era.

As with previous projects, I'm not really one to obsess over using expensive modern evenweave linens because such things didn't really exist in medieval times. I do what our medieval predecessors would have done and just choose a linen that looks reasonably even from the pile of linen I keep for making my medieval underwear, and I work with whatever linen thread I can find. I had some lovely medium-weight white linen thread stashed away

somewhere safe for this section of the book, but obviously I'd put it somewhere so safe I couldn't find it! So, instead, I completed this section with some random white thread I found on the internet, which was thinner so I had to double or quadruple it in places. Use what you have and have fun with it; if you can't find a nice white linen thread, use a perle cotton or white silk thread instead.

I've worked on a frame because it makes photography easier, but I suspect a lot of medieval whitework was done in hand, given the stitches used, so work in whichever way you find easiest.

In the case of the counted stitches, I have shown an expanded version for clarity alongside the proper version. I have also worked all of the samples in colour for contrast.

WHITEWORK TECHNIQUES

There is no single medieval whitework technique. There are separate counted and freehand versions, as well as pieces that combine both counted work and freehand. I suspect it was a case of using whatever stitches you knew in whatever combination gave a pleasing texture. Some surviving pieces are every bit as precise as modern Hardanger, whereas others take a looser, even downright sloppy approach.

Always remember to put on your trousers when walking the dog, no matter how hung over you happen to be.

Blanket Stitch

Sometimes also known as buttonhole stitch, this stitch can also be used to secure the edges of a piece of fabric, such as along a buttonhole or the edge of a blanket (hence the names). It is also often used as a decorative stitch in embroidery.

Fanned Blanket Stitch Variation

This variation is often used as a filling stitch in German whitework. It creates a great texture, which is valuable when working in monochrome.

Open Chain Stitch

Although regular chain stitch is found in medieval whitework, open chain is often favoured because it creates a broader line. It's worked with much the same structure as regular chain, but instead of pinching the anchoring stitches together, they're spaced a few millimetres apart.

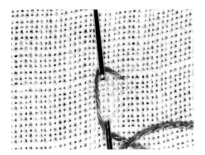

1 Anchor the end of your thread along the top edge of your intended line, then plunge the needle where you want the bottom edge to be. Come back up at the top, looping the thread around the needle so that it is held to the side by the next stitch.

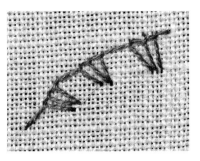

1 Start by working your stitches in groups of three with a gap between each group. Use a long connecting stitch between the groups of three to create a continuous – if somewhat lumpy – row.

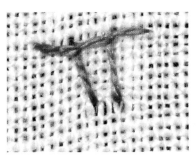

2 Repeat to make a row of open-armed stitches, securing the final loop with a holding stitch.

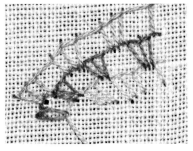

2 Work your next row of grouped stitches with the gaps in one row alternating with the bunched stitches of the next. You can work the row beneath by looping the connecting stitch through the bottom of the bunched stitches in the row above, or work the row above by working the bunched stitches over the connecting stitch of the group below. You may find one direction easier than the other; if you do you can plan your working direction around your preference.

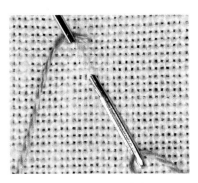

1 Start by bringing your stitch up where you want the top edge to be. Take it down along the bottom, then bring it back out at the top, while looping it around the thread.

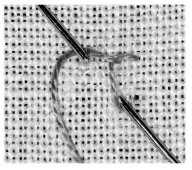

2 Take the thread back down at the bottom, using to pull the looped thread into place. This is a very flexible stitch and there's no right or wrong spacing between the loops – you can vary it to suit your design.

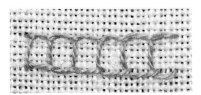

3 Repeat until your chain is the desired length. Secure the final loop with a small stitch, top and bottom.

Double German Brick Stitch

This stitch is exactly what it sounds like. It could be argued that this design was done with pattern darning, rather than counted satin and German brick stitches, but the original in the Deutschen Textilmuseums Krefeld clearly shows the sides pulling in to create clear gaps between the bands.

1 Follow German brick stitch (*see* Chapter 5), this time working a parallel pair of stitches before staggering them.

2 The rows can then be packed together to create texture.

Tulip Band

Mirroring the original diagonal on each side of the block makes a tulip shape.

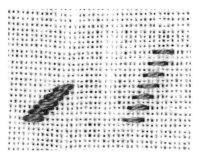

1 Start by working a row of six German brick stitches, each four rows of background canvas across from the bottom where you want the design to have an edge.

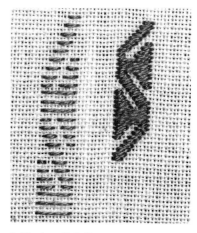

2 Work a stitch three rows across to make a flat edge. Throw three stitches out from the flat edge, each ten threads long. From the far edge of this block, work a descending series of stitches: five, four, three and two threads long, mirroring the original diagonal. Do this on each side of the block to make a tulip shape.

Work another row of brick stitches out to create the opposite leaf of the tulip. Then work the next tulip in the other direction.

Double Interlock Band

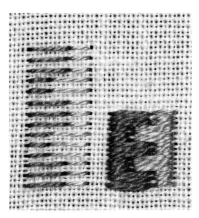

1 Work blocks of three stitches, four threads long, and alternate with blocks of three, eight threads long.

2 Work the same down the other side: a block of four next to every block of eight, and a block of eight next to each block of four.

Triple Interlock Band

This is just a more elaborate version of the double band.

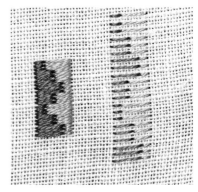

Work a block of three by three, followed by a block of three by six, then three by nine, three by six and three by three, up and down until the band reaches the desired length. Fill the opposite side in the same way.

German Braid Stitch

This is the most complicated of all the German counted stitches, but it is very pretty if you persevere. If I'm being honest, I have to check my notes every time to get this one right! It's worth remembering that this stitch is based on the same geometric principles as Celtic knotwork and the rhythmic border designs seen throughout medieval European art, so if you find yourself sitting there chanting 'under one, over one, under one, over one', you are not alone.

German braid stitch tends to be used for edges and framing borders rather than as a decorative filling. I'm going to be working a massively expanded two colour version for illustrative purposes, but I'll mention the usual spacing for the smaller counted version as I go along.

We start with a counted framework before going on to the top layer, which is worked freehand. It's a bit like one of those 'how do you draw a house with one continuous line' brain teasers.

Working as Individual Blocks

Here, German braid stitch is worked as individual blocks.

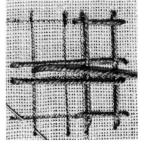

1 Work a grid, starting at the upper middle bar. For the real-size version, the first stitch should be fourteen threads across. Go diagonally across one stitch to change direction. The next stitch is five threads across at a right angle before changing direction to create a square in one corner.

2 Leap across the full length of your grid to create another square in the next corner.

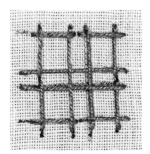

3 From there it's a pretty logical progression of repeating the same steps until you have a completed grid.

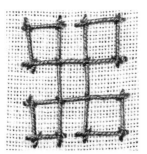

4 Honestly, I think the secret to success with this stitch is cheating. Once you start the braiding over the top of your grid, the braiding thread can slide around under the corners and make things very difficult, especially when you work to a smaller, more correct sort of scale. It can make life a lot easier if you tack the corners so the braiding can't slide under them (this isn't an authentic way to do it, I just find it a lot easier). It helps to use the finest white thread you have, so it becomes invisible.

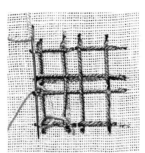

5 The braiding stitch is worked entirely on the surface, and should only pass through the ground fabric to start and finish. The rest is woven through the grid we just laid down.

Start at the inner corner by looping under the first inner bar, then over the upright and under the next upright. Work around the corners by remembering to go under and over. However, once you're heading upwards you need to go under two, so that when you work back over the centre you can continue the under-over rhythm.

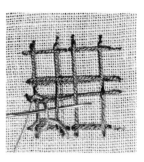

6 Once you've picked up the rhythm, you go under two again to leave room to impose the under-over repeat when you come back down.

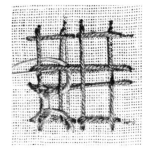

7 At this point, we abandon the first square with one side unfinished. Go up to the next square in the grid, repeating the first steps.

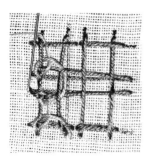

8 Remember again to go under two so that you leave room for the rhythm when you come back around the top corner.

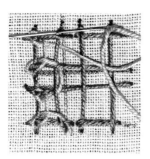

9 Then under two again. This time, instead of moving on to the next square, finish this by rounding the top corner.

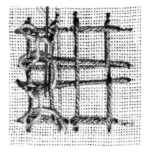

10 Pick up the middle thread in the continuing sequence. You might have to nudge the thread into place a bit. When you're working on a smaller scale, you might have to dig the middle thread out to pick it up properly.

11 Repeating the same sequence in the other two corner squares will create the same interwoven pattern in the middle. You can finish off the last side of the first square as the final step.

Working as a Continuous Diagonal

German braid stitch is commonly worked as a continuous diagonal. The braiding is done the same way because if you work around each grid the braiding won't join up.

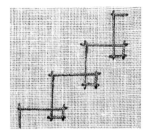

1 Work one side of the diagonal first.

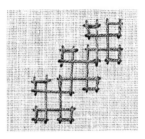

2 Turn around at the end and reverse the same sequence to make the other edge of the pattern.

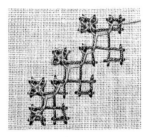

3 Work the braiding all the way up one side.

4 Turn around at the top and come back down the other side, As long you remember your unders and overs, it works exactly the same way. If you're working around a square shape, you would work all the way around the outside before tackling the inside.

WHITEWORK PROJECTS

Pussy Goes A-Hunting

Anthropomorphised images of vulvas and vaginas doing stuff are a running theme on pilgrim badges. They go on pilgrimage, are carried aloft by equally humanised phalluses and do all sorts of unlikely activities.

This design is a hybrid from two sources. The image is based on a pewter pilgrim badge, but the whitework treatment is based on a fragment of whitework in the collection of the Deutschen Textilmuseums Krefeld.

Materials

- Linen cloth, approx. 30cm (12in) square
- Crewel needle, size 22
- Linen thread: white and unbleached

Pussy goes a-hunting.

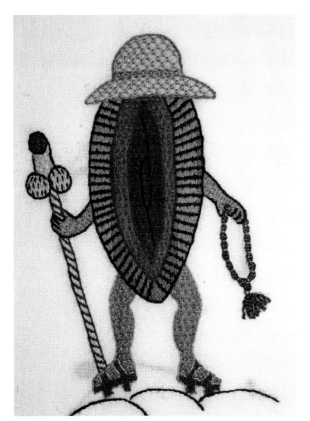

'The Pilgrim' and 'Queen V and the Pecker Parade' are based on pilgrim badges, like the pussy hunting image.

'The Lady Gardener' is my own design, because I always think the pilgrim looks as if she's wearing her gardening hat.

Template. Enlarge by 200%. Finished size 30cm (12in) square.

Transferring the Image

I have used a permanent fabric marker, but a fade-out pen would work well enough for this design as it is both washable and reasonably quick to do.

The Pony

With a body filled with double interlock and tulip patterns, the pony looks like he's wearing a chunky Aran-knit onesie.

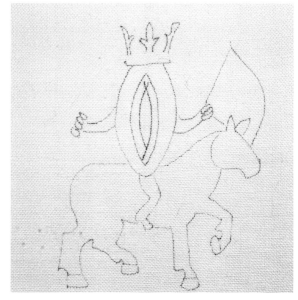

1 Transfer the design to your canvas.

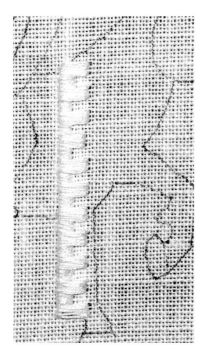

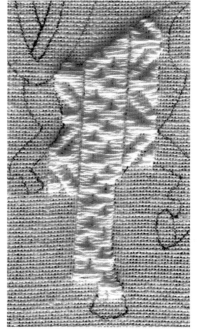

2 Start at the pony's hock (the heel of its foot). Work the first side of the double interlocking stitch up until you have filled the outline vertically. You may have to shape the edges of the band to fit the shape of the body.

3 Work the other side of the double interlocking band, again shaping it to fit within the outline.

4 Work bands of the tulip pattern on either side of the first band, using the same hole for the edges of each band. There should be no gaps between the two.

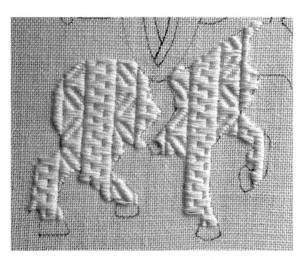

5 Fill the pony's body with alternating bands of double interlock and tulip pattern. Don't worry about the lines that delineate one leg from another; these will be added later.

6 Work the hooves and face of the pony in German brick stitch, as well as the points of pussy's crown.

Pussy

It can be hard to tell what is convent stitch and what is trailed couching in German whitework because sometimes it's worked straight and sometimes it goes all bendy, so just go with what feels right.

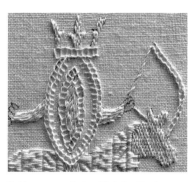

7 Use convent stitch for pussy's centre, legs and arms, as well as the bowstring.

8 Work around pussy's outer edge with blanket stitch to give the effect of pubic hair. I did the legs of my blanket stitch a little shorter than I originally intended to. I was going to pick it out and redo it, but when I did a second row of stitching I really liked the look of it so I decided to go with a double row instead. Either is fine.

9 Use open chain stitch for the inner circle on pussy, the band of her crown and her bow.

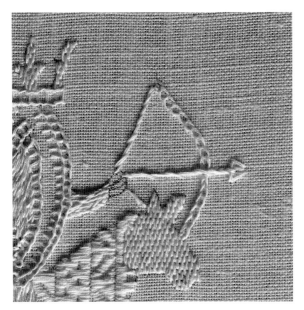

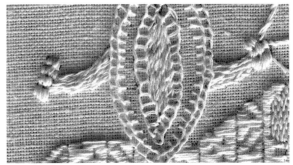

10 The arrow needs to be done in convent stitch, so it goes straight over the top of the bow.

11 Her fingers are just little clumps of satin stitch.

Outlining the Pony

Some German whitework introduces a touch of colour by using unbleached linen, and sometimes even a tiny bit of blue linen. (Linen is quite resistant to natural dyeing, and blue is the only colour that reliably works because it has a different dye process to most other dyes.)

12 Outline the pony using trailed couching in unbleached linen for a subtle contrast. It's at this stage that you delineate the legs and face of the pony. Don't forget to add some thongs to pussy's whip.

The Cobbled Street and Finishing Touches

Often, German braid stitch is used to create long diagonal lines by joining and stacking the blocks on their points (so you could enclose this design in a diamond of braid for a very medieval look). To create a straight line you could mark the blocks diagonally, but I like the effect of them stepping up and down to suggest a cobbled street.

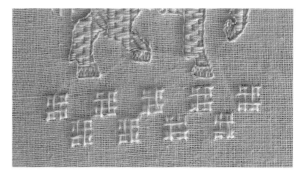

13 Add some blocks of German braid stitch to make a road beneath the pony's hooves. It will look better it you sew an odd number.

14 Once the braid part of braid stitch is done, she's ready to go a-hunting!

Mandrake

Mandrake – actually the dog is walking him!

Ben is a version of the Mandrake done in laid and couched work, with a fancy background based on those found in manuscripts.

The mandrake is a real plant. It was believed to have been generated when a hanged man ejaculated on the point of death, so obviously the idea of erotic asphyxiation is nothing new. When his 'seed' fell upon the ground below the gallows, the mandrake would sprout.

This strange homunculus-shaped root was thought to have numerous medicinal properties, from an aphrodisiac to a narcotic, but harvesting it was dangerous because it was believed to cry out when uprooted. Its cry was deadly to the first creature to hear it, so many herbals show the safe method of harvesting the valuable root. A dog was trained to sit and stay, then tied to the plant while the gardener retreated to a safe distance. When the dog was called, it ended up being the closest living thing to the deadly cry of the plant and the dog died. Obviously 'safe' is not a term applied to poor Fido, who was a soon to be ex-dog.

If you don't like that version you could always pretend that the mandrake is out taking his dog for a walk, because exercise is important – even for plants.

Materials

- Linen cloth, 30 × 40cm (12 × 16in)
- Crewel needle, size 22
- White linen thread

Transferring the Image

Note that, as with the Zodiac Man design (*see* Chapter 2), the ends of the hands and feet are left open and unmarked.

1 Mark the design out on the canvas. I've used a worn-out permanent fabric marker, which leaves only a faint line, but you could use a fade-out pen for this project, since it is both washable and reasonably quick to do.

Mandrake template. Enlarge by 200%. Finished size 30 × 40cm (12 × 16in).

The Dog

Don't worry about delineating the eyes and ears when stitching the head; that comes later

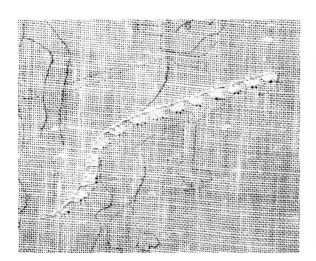

2 Work a line of fanned blanket stitch from the front of the dog's paw to the tip of his tail.

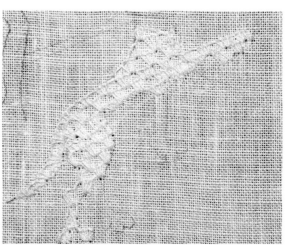

3 Fill out the rest of the dog's body from there, omitting the two legs at the far side of the body.

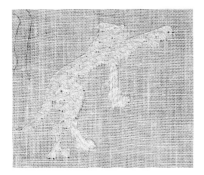

4 Work the other two legs in convent stitch.

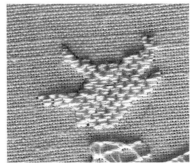

5 The dog's head is done in double German brick stitch.

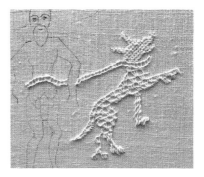

6 Use open chain stitch to chain the mandrake and dog together.

The Mandrake

Next move on to the mandrake's... leaves? Hair? Headdress? Who knows?

7 Fill the five leaves at the front of his little personal topiary with alternating triple interlock band and fanned buttonhole stitches.

8 Outline the rear leaves in blanket/buttonhole stitch.

9 Add central veins of open chain stitch.

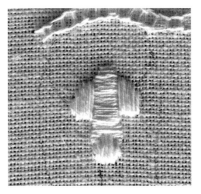

10 His rather large willy is worked in simple satin stitch, using two directions to distinguish the shaft and testicles. I won't tell him it looks like a cute little bumblebee, if you don't.

Outlining and Finishing Touches

There are parts of the dog where the upper part of the fanned blanket stitch creates its own outline, so, for instance, on his outstretched paw you only need to outline the bottom part, and it's the same along the dog's back.

11 Use trailed outline stitch/ curvy convent stitch for... well, for outlining, oddly enough.

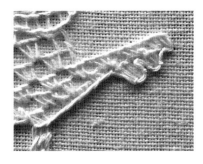

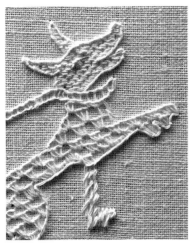

12 I don't think the convent stitch rear legs of the dog need to be outlined in a couched outline stitch that is really just a wavy version of convent stitch, so I've left them naked because it gives more sense of perspective. But use outline stitch to delineate the dog's ears and eye.

13 Where the toes and fingers have been left open, have some fun. Let them spread like roots, make them different lengths and add a few messy tendrils. Be organic rather than organised. Let his beard be messy as well.

14 Outline all of his body as well as the foremost leaves – the ones done in blanket stitch don't need an edge.

15 His face needs a slightly more delicate touch, so I've gone down from four strands to two and worked the features in stem stitch.

16 Now he's finished... and so is the dog, both literally and metaphorically.

SUPPLIERS

Crewel wool
https://appletons.org.uk

Naturally dyed crewel wool
https://mulberrydyer.com

Silk threads
https://devereyarns.co.uk
https://handweavers.co.uk

Gold threads
neil.halford@toye.com

For kits, bits and wool canvases
https://opusanglicanumembroidery.com

Slate frames
https://historyinthemaking.co.uk

Index

First published in 2024 by
The Crowood Press Ltd
Ramsbury, Marlborough
Wiltshire SN8 2HR

enquiries@crowood.com
www.crowood.com

British Library Cataloguing-in-Publication Data
A catalogue record for this book is available from the
British Library.

ISBN 978 0 7198 4347 1

Cover design by Su Richards

Graphic design and typesetting by Peggy & Co. Design
Printed and bound in India by Thomson Press India Ltd